Blackstone's Guide to the
FOOD SAFETY ACT 1990

Blackstone's Guide to the
FOOD SAFETY ACT 1990

Geraint G. Howells
Lecturer in the Unit for Commercial Law Studies, Sheffield University

J. Robert Bradgate
Lecturer in the Unit for Commercial Law Studies, Sheffield University

S. Margaret Griffiths
Senior Lecturer in Law, Polytechnic of Wales

BLACKSTONE
PRESS LIMITED

First published in Great Britain 1990 by Blackstone Press Limited,
9-15 Aldine Street, London W12 8AW. Telephone 081-740 1173

ISBN: 1 85431 108 5

British Library Cataloguing in Publication Data
A CIP catalogue record for this book is available from the British Library

Typeset by Style Photosetting Ltd, Mayfield, East Sussex
Printed by BPCC Wheatons Ltd, Exeter

Contents

Preface

Recently there have been numerous food scares about, among other things, salmonella, listeria, cook-chill foods, BSE and irradiated food. The Food Safety Act 1990 is not a direct response to these matters, although the controversies may have precipitated the timing of the reforms. Rather the Act is the result of a long-term review of food legislation and reflects the need to consolidate, modernise and strengthen the controls over food which had developed in a piece meal fashion.

The Act received broad support from industry, consumer groups and all political parties. However this masks divisions of opinion on some specific topics, notably the vexed question of whether irradiated food should be permitted. The business world is of course concerned that the burdens placed upon it are not too onerous, whilst consumer groups might question the wisdom of omitting a general safety duty. Both groups will await with interest the content of the regulations which will flesh out the framework established by the Act. In the meantime we hope this book will enable businesses, consumer groups and those with the responsibility for administering the Act to come to terms with the changes the Act has made and to help understand the future framework of food law.

The authors would like to thank the publishers for their enthusiasm for this project and the expeditious manner in which they transformed our typescript into the finished product. We would of course also like to thank our respective spouses for their support.

Geraint Howells
Robert Bradgate
Margaret Griffiths

Chapter One
Introduction

1.1 Historical perspective

Recent years have seen a massive increase in reported cases of food poisoning. According to statistics from the Communicable Diseases Surveillance Centre, there were 30,000 cases of food related illness in 1987, 41,000 cases in 1988 and over 54,000 cases in 1989. During that period there has been a series of highly publicised food 'scares', with problems of salmonella in eggs, listeria in cheese, cook-chill foods and bovine spongeform encephalopathy ('BSE') in beef, all receiving extensive media coverage. In 1988, 200 people died from salmonella poisoning. There is now a much greater public awareness of the problems of food safety. In that context it might be tempting to see the Food Safety Act 1990 as a response to a topical problem. However, the Act actually comes at the end of five years work involving an extensive review of existing food law.

There has been regulation of food content in England and Wales since the Assize of Bread and Ale of 1266. However, early legislation was largely concerned with fiscal matters. Modern food law is generally seen as consisting of two strands, the first concerned with adulteration and consumer protection, the second with public health. The first can be traced back to the Adulteration of Food and Drink Act 1860, whose provisions still form the basis for many of those in the new Act. It prohibited the sale of food to which materials or ingredients injurious to health had been added, and prohibited the sale of impure food. It was supplemented in 1872 by the Adulteration of Food and Drugs Act, which strengthened enforcement powers by requiring the appointment of public analysts and empowering local enforcement officers to take samples and bring prosecutions. In 1875 the Sale of Food and Drugs Act was passed, making it an offence to sell, to the prejudice of the customer, food not of the nature, quality or substance demanded by the customer. In the same year the Public Health Act 1875 introduced the second strand of food law, allowing local officers to take pre-emptive action by inspecting food and, if it appeared to be 'diseased or unsound or unwholesome or unfit for the food of man', to seize it and take it before a justice of the peace to be dealt with.

The first strand was consolidated and amended in 1928 by the Food and Drugs (Amendment) Act, and in 1938 a further consolidation, the Food Act 1938, brought the two strands together. The 1938 Act also made it an offence to apply false or misleading labels to food and contained power to make regulations governing the preparation, storage, sale etc. of food. Thus by 1938, most of the main elements of modern food law were in place. The Food and Drugs Act 1955 made some further amendments and re-consolidated the existing legislation, and the Food and Drugs (Scotland) Act 1956 and Food and Drugs (Northern Ireland) Act 1958 applied similar provisions to other parts of the UK. Further amendments were made and the English legislation was again consolidated in 1984 by the Food Act, although the 1956 and 1958 Acts remained in force in Scotland and Northern Ireland respectively.

1.2   Background to the 1990 Act

Almost immediately after passing the 1984 Act, the Government announced a full scale review of food law. An extensive programme of consultation, involving representatives of consumer, agricultural and business interests was initiated in December 1984. Several factors influenced the decision to undertake the review. Existing food law had remained largely unchanged since before the Second World War, and much of it dated from the Victorian era. However, considerable technological and social changes, particularly in the post-War period, had radically changed food production, retailing practices and consumer behaviour. Technological change led to the proliferation of food additives and the development of new methods of growing, preparing and processing food. At the same time, changes in social behaviour, combined with the widespread availability of prepared, processed and convenience foods, together with the growth of the supermarket, led to a massive increase in consumer demand for such pre-prepared and convenience foods. Although existing legislation contained powers to make regulations which might be used to try and keep pace with technological changes, it was felt that those powers were inadequate to deal with modern food production and preparation practices; nor were they always sufficient to enable the Government to comply with requirements imposed by membership of the European Community, which was playing an increasing role in food safety and regulation, and many EC obligations had to be met by regulations made under the European Communities Act of 1972 rather than under powers derived from food legislation.

At the same time, the proliferation of retail food outlets made it increasingly difficult for local authority enforcement officers to keep track of food businesses in their area. Some businesses were subject to a system of registration, but that only applied to particular categories of food business, notably those concerned with the manufacture or supply of ice-creams or sausages. It was therefore felt that some system of registration, or prior notification of the opening of food businesses, applicable to all types of food business, was necessary. In addition it was felt that there were loopholes in the pattern of offences created by existing legislation, and that enforcement powers were inadequate, especially for dealing with emergencies, when a closure order in respect of a business could only be made on three days notice.

Furthermore, the existing legislation was cluttered and disorganised. Three different statutes with broadly similar provisions applied in different parts of the UK, and whilst separate legislation for Northern Ireland is a constitutional requirement, it seemed unnecessary to have a separate Act for Scotland. Many types of food were subject to special regulation, often in primary legislation. Thus as noted above, special provisions applied in respect of ice-cream and sausages, and there was an extensive code (Part II of the 1984 Act, consisting of eighteen sections) applying only to milk and milk products.

1.3 Policy of the Act

In July 1989, following extensive consultation with various interested bodies, the Government published a White Paper, 'Food Safety — Protecting the Consumer', and announced its intention to introduce legislation at the earliest opportunity. The Food Safety Bill was introduced into the House of Lords on 22 November 1989. On the whole the Bill was relatively uncontroversial, and it passed into law largely unamended. Some items did provoke extensive debate, notably the inclusion of a provision to allow the irradiation of food, although it should be noted that the Act itself does not permit food irradiation, but allows the Minister to make regulations permitting the introduction of the process. On the other hand, many interested bodies, particularly consumer interest groups, have criticised the Act for what it omits.

The Bill was produced jointly by the Ministry of Agriculture, Fisheries and Food (MAFF) and the Department of Health, since the latter is responsible for public food hygiene and microbiological contamination. It is intended to build on the existing law to meet the new problems created by new techniques of food preservation and handling.

The Act aims to control all aspects of food safety throughout the food distribution chain. That chain starts not with the farmer or food producer, but at an earlier stage with the animal feed and agricultural chemical industries. Food safety can be affected by events at any stage of that chain, and for that reason it was felt that one Ministry (MAFF) should be responsible for all aspects of food safety throughout the chain. Consumer groups had demanded that food safety be dealt with separately from agricultural matters. In order to try to meet some of those demands, whilst retaining an integrated Ministry, in November 1989 the Minister established a Food Safety Directorate within the MAFF to divide food safety from food production responsibilities. At the same time a Consumer Panel was also established, to keep consumer interests under review.

The Act retains the main structure of offences concerned with food safety contained in the previous law, but seeks to revise those offences in order to tighten their definitions and fill several perceived lacunae in the law, as well as amending the defences available in prosecutions for those offences, and increasing penalties. At the same time it revises and improves the pre-emptive powers of enforcement, creating new powers to deal with emergencies. However, the declared aim of the Act is to strike a balance between consumer protection and 'the needs of an innovative and competitive food industry by avoiding unnecessary burdens and controls'. The striking of this balance is seen to be in the interests of both consumers and business.

Historically food law has been enforced by local officers and the tradition of local enforcement is continued by the new Act. However, local enforcement can lead to local disparities in the way the law is enforced. The Act therefore aims to minimise such disparities by providing for the Ministry to issue codes of practice for the guidance of local enforcement officers.

Finally the Act aims to procude a more streamlined but more flexible code of food safety law, by removing outdated or otiose provisions, repealing some of the special regulatory schemes for individual foods, and introducing new, wider powers to make regulations to meet the demands both of developments in food technology and of European Community membership.

1.4　　Outline of the Act

The main substance of the Act is in Part II, which contains the main offences and enforcement powers. The Act creates four offences concerned with food safety and consumer protection. They are closely based on offences established under the earlier law, but the chance has been taken to block a number of perceived gaps in the old law. Section 7 makes it an offence to render food injurious to health. Section 8 creates an offence of selling food which does not comply with food safety requirements: defined as food which is injurious to health, is unfit for human consumption or is contaminated; this section is considerably wider than the equivalent provision in the 1984 Act where there was felt to be a gap in consumer protection. Section 14 re-enacts the offence of selling food not of the nature, quality or substance demanded by the purchaser, and s. 15 creates an amended offence of falsely describing or presenting food; the reference to 'presentation' extends the protection given to the consumer, and was necessary to enable the Act to be used to comply with the EC Food Labelling Directive (79/112/EEC) which had been implemented using powers under the European Communities Act 1972.

The defences available to a person charged with an offence under the Act have been modified and revised. The statutory written warranty defence has been abolished, but a defence of 'due diligence' has been created. Penalties for convicted offenders have been increased.

Part II also revises and strengthens the administrative and enforcement powers exercisable to promote food safety. Local authority enforcement officers have power to inspect and seize unsafe food (s. 9), to serve improvement notices (s. 10) and to obtain prohibition orders to enforce food hygiene regulations (s. 11). There is also power to obtain a prohibition order against a named individual, preventing such person being involved in any food business. New powers are given to both local authorities and the Minister to deal with emergencies. Where there is an imminent risk to health due to breach of hygiene regulations, the local authority enforcement officer has power to serve an emergency prohibition notice, effective immediately, and to apply to the court for an emergency prohibition order, on giving one day's notice (s. 12); previously emergency action could only be taken on application to the court, and on three day's notice. There is also a new power for the Minister to make an 'emergency control order' where urgent action is needed to deal with a more widespread problem not confined to a particular locality (s. 13). Although it is anticipated that such problems will continue to be dealt with on the basis of voluntary co-operation between the food businesses affected and the Minister, this will be an important power for use in emergencies.

Enforcement is further strengthened by an important new provision in s. 8 which provides that where any food which fails to comply with a food safety requirement forms part of a batch, lot or consignment, the whole batch (etc) is rebuttably presumed to be similarly affected, allowing the enforcement authority to seize (etc) the whole batch, unless any part of it can be shown to be safe. In such situations in the past it has been necessary to rely on voluntary co-operation.

Many matters of detail will be dealt with by regulations. There is extensive power for the Minister to make regulations covering a wide range of matters (s. 16; sch. 1), including any regulations necessary to comply with European Community commitments (s. 17). In recognition of the growing importance of technological advances in food production there is further power to make regulations to deal with 'novel foods' (s. 18). The considerable body of delegated legislation made under the 1955 and 1984 Acts remains in force.

Section 19 empowers the Ministers to make regulations requiring the registration or licensing of premises used for the purposes of food businesses. These provisions will be particularly useful to enforcement authorities: a comprehensive register of premises used for the purposes of food businesses will assist them in keeping track of local food businesses. Licensing would allow the enforcement authority to exercise pre-emptive control. However, the power to make regulations requiring licensing may only be exercised for limited purposes and so a comprehensive licensing system is unlikely to be introduced.

Training for those involved in the production, preparation, packaging or handling of food has been seen as an important weapon in the battle against food related illness. The Act therefore permits enforcement authorities to provide training courses in food hygiene for such persons (s. 23). Furthermore the Minister is empowered to make regulations requiring persons who are, or intend to be, involved in the food business to undergo food hygiene training (sch. 1 para 5).

The policy of seeking uniformity of enforcement is implemented by s. 40 which allows the Minister to issue codes of practice on the execution and enforcement of the Act and regulations made under it. Enforcement authorities are required to have regard to any relevant code in exercising their functions under the Act or regulations.

In line with the declared aim of simplifying and streamlining the legislation, the special provisions applying to milk and milk products, previously in the Food Act 1984, ss. 32–49 are repealed and not replaced. Instead, milk is now dealt with under the general provisions applicable to all food or, where there are specific problems relating to milk or milk products, under appropriate regulations.

The 1984 Act also contained detailed provisions, in ss. 76–86 and sch 7 governing sampling and analysis procedures. It was felt that many of those provisions were inappropriate for inclusion in primary legislation and would be better dealt with in regulations. The new Act contains just five sections (ss. 27–31) governing analysis and sampling, with power in s. 31 for the Minister to make regulations dealing with matters of detail.

The Act and regulations made under it are binding on the Crown (s. 54), and although the Crown may not be held criminally liable under the Act, the High Court or, in Scotland, the Court of Session, may declare unlawful any act or omission of the Crown which constitutes a contravention of the Act. Immunity from criminal liability applies only to the Crown itself: individuals in the public service of the Crown are subject to the same liability under the Act as other individuals; thus where an offence may have been committed by an individual, the latter can be prosecuted. Enforcement powers can be exercised in respect of property and activities of the Crown, although there is power for the Secretary of State to issue a certificate preventing the exercise of powers of entry in respect of any Crown premises specified in the certificate where it appears to him requisite or expedient in the interests of national security so to do.

Overall the new Act is considerably more streamlined than its predecessors, running to 60 sections and five schedules, compared with 136 sections and 11 schedules in the 1984 Act. It applies to the whole of Great Britain, repealing the whole of the 1956 Act and the 1984 Act apart from Parts III (Markets) and V (Sugar Beet and Cold Stores) and certain related enforcement provisions, which remain in force as amended. A number of other Acts are also amended, including the Food and Environment Protection Act 1985, the Water Act 1989 and the Water (Scotland) Act 1989. With certain exceptions (see s. 60(5)) the Act does not apply to Northern Ireland. Sections 13, empowering the Minister to make emergency control orders, and 51, amending the Food and Environment Protection Act 1985, and Sch. 2, paras 12–15 amending the provisions of the Food Act 1984 relating to sugar beet and cold storage and s. 52 so far as relating to those paragraphs, come into force immediately; the remaining provisions of the Act are to be brought into force by Ministerial order on such day or days as the Minister may appoint (s. 60). The bulk of the Act is likely to be in force by 1 January 1991, but it is expected that registration of food premises under s. 19 will not be introduced until 1 April 1991, and s. 23, which permits food authorities to provide training for food handlers, will come into force on 1 July 1991. Section 54, which abrogates Crown immunity, is not likely to be brought into force until 1 April 1992.

1.5   Areas of controversy

Although the new Act does a great deal to improve existing food safety law it has been criticised, particularly by consumer lobby groups, for a number of reasons. Four in particular are worth mentioning here. First, the Act does not introduce a comprehensive licensing system. Many commentators, and some representatives of environmental health officers, would have preferred such a system to be introduced, particularly if the grant of a licence were to be linked to a basic training requirement so as to provide a measure of pre-emptive control, particularly over new food businesses.

Secondly, the Act creates an offence of selling food which fails to comply with safety requirements. However, 'safety requirements' are defined in precise terms and, despite several attempts to amend the Bill in Parliament, the Act does not contain a general safety requirement. Such a requirement applies to other classes of product under the Consumer Protection Act 1987 (s. 10) which requires goods to be reasonably safe having regard to all the circumstances, and similar general duties are also imposed under the Health and Safety at Work Act 1974. The Consumers' Association, amongst others, would have favoured the imposition of such a general safety requirement in relation to food, in order to catch possible cases falling outside the existing definition of 'safety requirements' and not covered by specific regulations. If the EEC draft Directive on Product Safety becomes law it will extend a general safety requirement to food.

Thirdly, there has been strong lobbying for the imposition of a system of nutritional labelling and some lobbyists hoped that the chance would be taken to impose such a system in the new Act. No such system is created by the Act itself, although it would seem that the Ministers' powers to make regulations are sufficiently wide to allow such a system to be created by secondary legislation. In any case, nutritional labelling is under consideration by the European Community which is likely to give a lead in this area.

Finally, many consumer groups have urged the creation of a distinct consumer or food ministry to ensure that consumer interests are kept separate from those of food producers. As already noted, the view of the Government is that a co-ordinated approach to food law can best be achieved within a unitary Ministry.

1.6   Enforcement and the division of powers

Responsibility for enforcing the new Act is divided between local and central government. Most provisions are to be enforced by food authorities, as defined in s. 5, acting through their authorised officers. The food authority will be a different authority in different parts of the country. (See generally chapter 7, infra.)

Food authorities are responsible for enforcing the main criminal provisions of the Act (ss. 7, 8, 14 and 15), for exercising the enforcement powers in ss. 9–12 and for enforcing regulations made under the Act. They will also be responsible for maintaining any register of food premises under s. 19 and may also provide food hygiene training (s. 23) and facilities for cleansing shellfish (s. 24).

Certain powers are retained to be exercised by Ministers. In most cases the relevant Minister is the Ministry of Agriculture, Fisheries and Food (MAFF) or the Secretary of State for Scotland (s. 4(1)); certain powers, including the power to make regulations under s. 16, are exercisable jointly by the MAFF and the Secretary of State concerned with health. In addition to the power to make regulations, the Minister may issue emergency control orders under s. 13. He also retains a supervisory jurisdiction over enforcement authorities,

which may be exercised in a number of ways. He may issue codes of practice
(s. 40) to which enforcement authorities must have regard in the exercise of
their functions and directions requiring a food authority to comply with the
provisions of any such code (s. 40(2)(b)).

The Minister may require a food authority to send him reports and returns
about the exercise of its functions (s. 41) and if a food authority is in default
by failing to discharge any duty imposed on it by the Act, he may make an
order allowing another food authority or one of his officers to take over the
discharge of that duty from the authority in default (s. 42).

The Act considerably extends the range of duties imposed on local authorities as food authorities. It is expected that the enforcement of the new
provisions will involve a substantial increase in spending in this area. The
Financial Memorandum accompanying the Food Safety Bill estimated the
likely increase at £30 million and the Government is pledged to take that sum
into account in fixing the Revenue Support Grant for 1991–2. Fears have been
expressed that this sum may prove inadequate: it is necessarily an estimate and
local authorities estimate that the sum required will be closer to £40 million.
It is not yet clear how the extra money will be made available, nor how it will
be distributed.

The exercise of the new functions under the Act will also mean an increase
in the requirements for both clerical staff and trained officers to carry out
enforcement functions. Food authorities will generally act through 'authorised
officers', who will be required to possess such qualifications as may be required
by regulations (s. 5(6)). In general it seems likely that food authorities will
exercise most of their functions through environmental health officers or
trading standards officers. Concern has also been expressed about the ad-
equacy of the supply of places on training courses, and therefore of the supply
of suitably trained personnel to police the new Act. Ultimately the success or
failure of the new law will depend on adequate resources being made available
to ensure proper enforcement.

Chapter Two
The Scope of the Act

2.1 'Food'

The Food Safety Act 1990 is concerned with the safety of food. Many of the main substantive provisions of the Act, contained in Part II, relate to 'food'. Thus, for instance, it is an offence to render food injurious to health (s. 7); to sell food which does not comply with food safety requirements (s. 8); to sell food which is not of the nature, substance or quality demanded by the purchaser (s. 14) or to sell food under a misleading or false description (s. 15). What is 'food' for the purposes of the Act?

'Food' is partly defined by s. 1, which sets out a list of items which are included in the definition (s. 1(1)) and a second list of items which are excluded (s. 1(2)).

Section (1) provides that the following are included in the definition of 'food'.

(a) Drink. It would seem that any drink is covered by the Act, including water. This was necessary in order to ensure that bottled mineral waters would be covered by the Act. However, account must be taken of ss. 55–6 which provide that the provisions of Part II of the Act (including all the main offences and powers of inspection, seizure etc) do not apply to the supply of water to premises, either by a water undertaker or by means of a private supply. Instead, the supply of water to premises is governed by the Water Act 1989 (or, in Scotland, by the Water (Scotland) Act 1990), which are amended to apply to the supply of water for domestic 'or food production purposes'. 'Food production purposes' are defined by the Water Act 1989, s. 1A, inserted by the 1990 Act, s. 55(6), and the Water (Scotland) Act 1990, s. 1A, inserted by s. 56(6), as 'manufacturing, processing, preserving or marketing purposes with respect to food or drink for which water supplied to food production premises may be used'. The result is that the supply of water to the tap is governed by the provisions of the Water Acts; but that once the water has been drawn from the tap it falls to be regulated by the Food Safety Act. Take the following example. A customer in a restaurant asks for a glass of water. The water is contaminated with insect larvae as a result of contamination of the local reservoir. The restaurant commits an offence under s. 8 or s. 14 of the Act. However, since the water was supplied from the mains in contaminated form, the restaurant will probably be able to rely on the due diligence defence contained in s. 21 of the Act unless there was reason to know of the contamination before serving the customer. The water supply company, on the other hand, may be liable under the Water Acts, but not under the Food Safety Act.

(b) 'Articles and substances of no nutritional value which are used for human consumption' (s. 1(1)(b)). This would seem to include food additives, colourings and the like (which may also be covered by s. 1(1)(d), below) and dietary supplements.

(c) Chewing gum and similar products (s. 1(1)(c)).

(d) Articles and substances used as ingredients in the preparation of food, or of the articles listed in paras. (a), (b) and (c) above (s. 1(1)(d)).

Section 1(2) then lists the following items which are expressly excluded from the definition of 'food'. Most are the subject of separate regulatory systems, although in some cases certain provisions of the Food Safety Act may apply to them as will appear below.

(a) Live animals (which includes all living creatures other than birds or fish: thus it would include edible insects) or birds are never 'food'; nor are live fish, except those which are used for human consumption whilst alive. 'Fish' is defined by s. 53 to include crustaceans and molluscs, so that edible snails are fish for this purpose. Where fish, such as oysters, are eaten alive, they are 'food'.

(b) Fodder or feeding stuffs for animals, birds or fish. Thus it would not be an offence under the Food Safety Act to sell cattle food contaminated with lead, even though that might result in contaminated milk entering the food chain. However, animal food is regulated under seprate provisions, and it would seem that some of the powers to make regulations (s. 16) and to make emergency control orders (s. 13) in the Food Safety Act might apply to animal feeding stuffs.

(c) Controlled drugs within the meaning of the Misuse of Drugs Act 1971.

(d) Medicines as defined in the Medicines Act 1968, and other articles or substances licensed pursuant to orders made under that Act. Previous legislation covered food and drugs together, but medicines and drugs are now regulated separately and were excluded from the 1984 Act. Note that certain health foods and dietary supplements sold in the form of pills or tablets are not classed as medicines and therefore fall within the definition of food in the 1990 Act.

2.2 'Articles' and 'substances'

Both s. 1(1)(b) and 1(1)(d) refer to 'articles or substances'. Both words are defined by s. 53. 'Article' is not expressly defined but is said to include a live animal or bird, or a live fish (which includes crustaceans and molluscs) which is not used for human consumption while it is alive, thus ensuring that live creatures are not indirectly included in the defintion of 'food'. 'Substance' includes 'any natural or artificial substance or other matter', whether in solid, liquid, gaseous or vapour form. That wide definition ensures that all the additives currently used in food manufacture, both natural and chemical, including flavourings, colourants, anti-oxidants, emulsifiers etc, are within the definition of 'food'.

2.3 Wider applications

Food safety may be affected by matters not concerned with the food itself. Some provisions of the Act therefore have a wider application than merely to 'food' as defined. Thus under s. 13 the Minister has power to make 'emergency control orders' in respect of food, food sources or contact materials. Similarly, regulations may be made under s. 16 in respect of food, food sources or contact materials. The powers under ss. 10–12 to serve improvement or prohibition notices are exercisable in relation to a 'food business' and, for the purposes of enforcement, samples may be taken of food, food sources and contact materials (s. 29). The inclusion of 'food sources' and 'contact materials' reflects the Government's concern to apply control throughout the food distribution chain.

2.3.1   Food sources
'Food source' is defined by s. 1(3) as 'any growing crop or live animal, bird or fish from which food is intended to be derived'. Food may be derived from a 'food source' by any means, including harvesting, slaughtering, milking or collecting eggs. Thus live cattle infected by BSE would not be 'food' but would be a 'food source' and there would be power to make regulations or emergency control orders governing their use etc. The defintion of 'food source' also enables some of the Act's provisions to be extended to cover premises where businesses sell poultry live to the consumer for slaughter and dressing on the premises after sale; this situation was previously beyond the ambit of food hygiene requirements.

2.3.2   Contact materials
The ambit of the Act is further extended by the definition of 'contact materials' as 'any article or substance which is intended to come into contact with food'. Thus crockery and cutlery would be included, together with serving implements (e.g. ice cream scoops) and packaging materials. Regulations could therefore be made, for instance, to restrict the use of certain types of plastic wrap in order to prevent the migration to food of possibly carcinogenic chemicals. The extension to contact materials is necessary to allow the UK fully to implement the EC Directive on materials and articles intended to come into contact with food (EC Directive 76/893/EEC).

2.3.3   Food business
'Food business' is also widely defined. By s. 1(3) a food business is any business in the course of which commercial operations are carried out with respect to

food or food sources. 'Business' includes activities which would normally be regarded as non-commercial, including the undertaking of a canteen, club, school, hospital or institution and activities or undertakings carried on by a local or public authority. Such activities are still a 'business' even though not carried on for profit.

2.3.4 Commercial operations

The essence of the definition of 'food business' threfore appears to be the carrying on of 'commercial operations'. Commercial operations may be carried on in relation to food, contact materials and food sources. Commercial operations include:

(a) The sale (etc), consignment for sale, preparation for sale (including processing, treatment and packaging — s. 53) of food or contact materials.
(b) Presentation (other than advertising or labelling — s. 53) for sale of food or contact materials.
(c) Storing or transporting for sale of food or contact materials.
(d) Importing or exporting of food or contact materials.
(e) Deriving food from a food source for the purpose of sale or any related purpose.

The result would seem to be that any type of business, profit making or otherwise, involved at any stage of the food production and delivery chain, from farm or factory right up to the delivery of food to the consumer, is a 'food business' and therefore subject to at least some of the regulatory powers contained in the Act.

2.4 'Sale'

Many of the offences created by the Food Safety Act are committed when food is sold for human consumption: e.g. selling food which fails to comply with food safety requirements (s. 8), selling food not of the nature, quality or substance demanded (s. 14) or selling food with a false or misleading description (s. 15). In addition, the powers of inspection, seizure and condemnation of food (s. 9) arise where food is sold. In some cases an offence is also committed by doing specified acts preparatory to sale, such as:—

(a) Offering or exposing the food (etc) in question for sale (ss. 8, 9, 15); the inclusion of 'exposure for sale' is necessary because of the restricted, contractual meaning given to 'offer' in cases such as *Fisher* v *Bell* [1961] 1 QB 394 where it was held that the display of goods in a shop does not amount in law to an offer to sell them.
(b) Advertising the food for sale (s. 8).
(c) Possessing the food (etc) for the purposes of sale (ss. 8, 9, 15) or for preparation for sale (ss. 8, 9) or
(d) Consigning the food to or depositing it with another person for the purposes of a sale (ss. 8, 9).

The scope of the Act is further widened by s. 2 which extends the meaning of 'sale' to include any other supply in the course of a business and any other thing done to food if specified in an order by the Minister. The phrase 'in the course of a business' appears in several other pieces of legislation, some concerned with consumer protection. Its meaning has been considered in the context of the Trade Descriptions Act 1968 (see *Davies* v *Sumner* [1984] 3 All ER 831) and the Unfair Contract Terms Act 1977 (*R&B Customs Brokers Ltd* v *United Dominion Trust Ltd* [1988] 1 All ER 847) where it has been held that a sale or purchase of goods is only 'in the course of business' if either the transaction is integral to the activities of the business (such as a sale of stock in trade) or there is some degree of regularity of similar transactions. A similar line may be taken in interpreting the phrase under the Food Safety Act, although note must be taken of the meaning of 'business' in s. 1. Reading the two sections together, it would seem that, inter alia, a supply of a meal to a patient by a hospital, a supply of free school meals to school children and the provision of free canteen facilities by an employer to its employees are all to be construed as 'sales'. Additionally, s. 2(2) provides that where food is offered as a prize, it is treated as being offered for sale. The result appears to be that almost any supply of food, whether for profit or otherwise, is a sale, with the exceptions of an occasional or one-off supply or a purely domestic supply, for instance to guests at a dinner party, or a charitable gift by an individual.

2.5 'Human consumption'

Where the Act creates offences or enforcement powers in the event of a sale (etc) or some preparatory act, the sale in question must generally be a sale for human consumption. However, by virtue of s. 3 it is presumed that if food commonly used for human consumption is sold (etc) the sale was for human consumption. This repeats a provision previously contained in the Food Act 1984 s. 98. It is an important presumption, since in many cases it would be difficult if not impossible for an enforcement authority to prove that a sale was for human consumption. The presumption created by s. 3 is rebuttable, but it will be for the defendant charged with a sale-related offence to call evidence to satisfy the court and displace the presumption. Similar rebuttable presumptions apply to:

(a) Food commonly used for human consumption which is found on premises used for the preparation, storage or sale of such food (s. 3(3)(a)).

(b) Any article or substance commonly used in the manufacture of food used for human consumption found on premises where such food is prepared, stored or sold (s. 3(3)(b)).

(c) Any article or substance capable of being used in the composition or preparation of food and found on premises where such food is prepared (s. 3(4)).

Chapter Three
Food Safety

3.1 Introduction

As noted in Chapter 1, there has been general food safety legislation since the Adulteration of Food and Drink Act of 1860. Part II of the 1990 Act, containing a number of provisions concerned with food safety and purity, draws on that earlier legislation. It creates criminal liability for making food injurious to health and for selling unsafe food, supplemented by extensive powers for local authority officers and the Minister to serve notices and make orders controlling and restricting the activities of particular businesses or more widespread commercial operations which create a risk of injury to health.

3.2 Overview of food safety provisions

The main food safety provisions are contained in ss. 7–13 of the Act, but they are closely linked to and suplemented by the extensive powers, contained in sections 16 and 26, to make regulations.

The principle criminal offences are created by ss. 7 and 8. Section 7 makes it an offence to render food injurious to health; s. 8 creates a series of offences concerned with the sale of food which fails to comply with a 'food safety requirement'.

Section 9–13 contain supplementary administrative and enforcement powers to be exercised by food authority enforcement officers and the Minister. Section 9 gives enforcement officers the power to inspect food and seize food which fails to conform to safety requirements. Section 10 and 11 empower enforcement officers to serve improvement notices and to apply to the court for prohibition orders in the event of breach of certain classes of regulations, and s. 12 gives the enforcement officer power to serve emergency prohibition notices and to apply for emergency prohibition orders. The powers in ss. 11 and 12 are exercisable where a 'health risk condition' is fulfilled by reason of there being a risk of injury to health. Finally, s. 13 gives the Minister power to make emergency control orders in respect of any commercial operations involving imminent risk of injury to health.

3.3 Injury to health

The concept of 'injury to health' is central to the provisions of ss. 7–13 and the regulation making powers in ss. 16 and 26. It is the core of the offence in s. 7, and food which is injurious to health fails to comply with food safety requirements for the purpose of s. 8. The two concepts of 'injury to health' and failure to comply with food safety requirements in turn trigger the enforcement powers in ss. 9–13.

'Injury to health' is defined in s. 7(3) as 'any impairment, whether permanent or temporary', and 'injurious to health' is to be construed accordingly. In deciding whether food is injurious to health, s. 7(2) provides that regard is to be had:

(a)   not only to the probable effect of that food on the health of a person consuming it; but

(b)   also to the probable cumulative effect of food of substantially the same composition on the health of a person consuming it in ordinary quantities.

This direction, to have regard to both the immediate effect of the food in question and to the long-term effects of consumption of similar food, reproduces a similar provision in s. 1(4) of the Food Act 1984. However, it seems that s. 7(2) only applies to s. 7 and to the definition of 'food safety requirements' in ss. 8 and 9.

It would appear that 'injury to health' could include food allergies and intolerances, coronary heart disease caused by consumption of saturated fats, and dental caries. It seems that the definition is intended to reflect existing case law. In the context of allergic and intolerant reactions, the words 'a person consuming it' in s. 7(2) are crucial. The court is directed to the effect of the food on a hypothetical consumer, not a particular individual who may have eaten food. Thus if the food in question produces a rare allergic reaction in a very small minority of cases it is probably not injurious to health. This reflects the law laid down in *Cullen* v *McNair* (1908) 72 JP 280 where it was said that food was not injurious merely because 'some exceptional individual is liable to have some particular injury done to his health'; however, if a significant proportion of the public are likely to be adversely affected, the food will be injurious. Thus in *Cullen* v *McNair,* cream treated with boracic acid as a preservative, which was perfectly safe to healthy adults but would adversely affect invalids or young children, was injurious. A food which caused an allergic reaction in a significant proportion of the population could therefore be regarded as injurious.

Similarly, food will not be regarded as 'injurious' merely because it can create adverse effects if consumed in excessive quantities. A hangover due to over indulgence in alcoholic drink might well be regarded as an 'injury to health' but the drink in question would not be regarded as injurious. This may be important in the light of the reference in s. 7(2) to cumulative effects. Modern health and nutritional research frequently reveals that common food stuffs eaten over a period of time may have a serious adverse effect on health: for instance, saturated fats increase the risk of heart disease, sugars of dental caries and salt of high blood pressure and consequential illness. Section 7(2) might therefore allow, for example, chips fried in saturated fat to be regarded as injurious to health and allow the chip vendor to be prosecuted if the chips were injurious when consumed in 'ordinary quantities'. It is worth bearing in mind that there is evidence that diet may vary according to social, economic and geographical factors so that 'ordinary quantities' may vary from place to place. Thus it might be possible, in an area of high chip consumption, to establish that eating ordinary quantities of chips fried in saturated fat would be injurious to health. However, as already noted, s. 7(2) repeats provisions contained in existing legislation, where such problems do not appear to have arisen. It is to be expected that the section will be interpreted in a common sense way both by enforcement authorities and by courts. Moreover, in view of the existing demands on their time and the problems posed by more imminent health risks, enforcement officers are unlikely to seek to utilise their powers under Part II of the Act to raise health and nutritional standards, especially when such action would rely upon expert opinion which is frequently contradictory.

With regard to newly discovered health risks, it is worth observing that although there is no 'state of the art defence' available in proceedings under food safety provisions, there is a due diligence defence which would presumably be available to a food manufacturer or supplier etc who had followed currently accepted standards and prevailing expert opinion.

Section 7(2) is not expressly applied to the enforcement powers in ss. 11–13. This could mean that long-term health risks created by cumulative consumption of a food cannot be taken into account in order to trigger the enforcement powers in those sections. However, in the context of the relevant sections, the concept of 'injurious to health' is probably sufficiently flexible to take account of cumulative effects without the specific reference in s. 7(2).

3.4   Rendering food injurious to health

Section 7 creates a specific offence of rendering food injurious to health with intent that it shall be sold for human consumption, reproducing the offence previously contained in the Food Act 1984, s. 1. The offence may be committed in any of four ways, namely by:

   (a)   adding any article or substance to the food;
   (b)   using any article or substance as an ingredient in the preparation of the food;
   (c)   abstracting any constituent from the food; or
   (d)   subjecting the food to any other process or treatment.

'Article', 'substance' and 'preparation' are all defined in s. 53 of the Act; the meanings of 'article' and 'substance' have been considered at 2.2, above. 'Preparation' is widely defined to include manufacture, and 'any form of processing or treatment', and 'treatment' is in turn defined as including subjecting the food to hot or cold. There might be scope for argument as to whether additives and colourings are truly 'ingredients', but in view of the wide definition of 'preparation' it is submitted that they are. If not, they would clearly fall within the category of articles or substances added to food in para. (a). 'Process' is not defined; the word is also used in a similar context in the Consumer Protection Act 1987. It has been suggested that a process must be a 'continuous and regular operation', although the House of Lords has recently held, in a different context, that a process can include any operation or series of operations carried on over a period of more than minimal duration, even if not repeated, provided there is some degree of continuity over a period of time (*Nurse* v *Morganite Crucible Ltd* [1989] 1 All ER 113, a case on the Factories Act 1961 and Asbestos Regulations 1969). In the Parliamentary debates on the Consumer Protection Act 1987 it was suggested that a process must alter some essential characteristic of the food product. However, it is thought that this may be too restrictive and that in the context of legislation concerned with consumer protection and public safety a court would give a wide and natural meaning to 'process' to include such activities as slaughtering food animals, pasteurising milk, canning and bottling, and so on, and perhaps even washing vegetables.

In recent years concern has been expressed about the effects of chemicals used to treat fruit and vegetables. Citrus fruit are often treated with a wax chemical spray after picking; the long term effects of such sprays and their residues are unknown. Such treatment would appear to be capable of giving rise to liability under para. (a), (b) or (d) if the wide definition of 'process' suggested above is accepted. Simiarly, the spraying of crops before harvesting may also give rise to liability: the definition of 'food' in s. 1 excludes live animals etc, but not growing crops, although both live animals and growing crops are included within the definition of 'food source'. Thus it would seem that, for instance, spraying apples with alar or similar chemicals could fall within either para. (a) or para. (d) and give rise to liability if it is shown that the spray has harmful effects, either in the short or long term. Whilst a prosecution might be unlikely in such a case, the section would appear to permit it and the defendant would have to rely on the due diligence defence in s. 21.

Another area of concern in recent years has been the problem of food sabotage by various groups and individuals; for instance, glass and other dangerous substances have been found added to baby food. Such a saboteur would clearly commit an offence under s. 7 and could be prosecuted if identified, although in practice other criminal offences are also likely to have been committed. However, s. 7 has a much wider ambit, and it should be noted that the offence created is one of strict liability insofar as it may be committed even though the defendant had no intention to render the food injurious to health. Thus it may be committed even though the additive or process in question was not known by the defendant to be injurious, subject to the due diligence defence. On the other hand the section does require a specific intent that the food should be sold for human consumption. The meaning of 'intent' in the general criminal law is unclear. Generally, if a defendant can be shown to have foreseen something as the natural and probable consequence of his actions, he will be taken to have intended that consequence. However, the problems of defining and proving intent in the present context are mitigated by the rebuttable presumption in s. 3 that food commonly used for human consumption, and articles or substances commonly used in the manufacture of food for human consumption, are intended for such sale or use if sold, offered, exposed or kept for sale, or found on premises used for the preparation, storage, or sale of such food. This reverses the burden of proof (see 2.5).

3.4.1   Abstracting
The offence in s. 7 can be committed by 'abstracting a constituent' from food as well as by adding things to food. Case law indicates that a constituent can be abstracted by (for instance) evaporation. Thus in *Bridges* v *Griffin* [1925] 2 KB 233 cream was held to have been abstracted from fresh milk when the milk was allowed to stand unstirred in its container, so that the cream rose to the top. Milk was dispensed from a tap at the bottom of the container. It was held that the cream had been abstracted from the milk sold, even though the milk was in the same condition in which it came from the cow.

3.4.2   Failure to process
The offence created by s. 7 does appear to leave one loophole. Although an offence is committed if things are added or subtracted from the food, and by subjecting the food to a process or treatment, no offence is committed by failing to subject the food to a necessary process or treatment. Thus, for instance, a failure to cook red kidney beans adequately can leave powerful and even deadly toxins in the beans; a failure adequately to cook canned beans prior to canning would not give rise to an offence under s. 7. However, the sale (etc) of such beans would be an offence under s. 8.

A person convicted on indictment of an offence under s. 7 may be sentenced to up to two years imprisonment and/or a fine. If convicted summarily, the maximum penalty is a £20,000 fine and/or a period of up to six months imprisonment (s. 35).

3.5   Selling food not complying with food safety requirements

Section 8 imposes a food safety requirement and creates a series of offences concerned with the sale etc, of food which fails to comply with that requirement. The section replaces offences previously contained in the 1984 Act ss. 1 and 8, but substantially expands the ambit of criminal liability. Indeed, the expressed intention behind ss. 7 and 8 of the new Act was to bridge a perceived gap in the liability created by the 1984 Act ss. 1, 2(a) and 8. Nevertheless, despite this widening of liability, the new Act does not impose a general safety requirement in relation to food, in contrast to the general safety requirement imposed on other products by Part II of the Consumer Protection Act 1987. This has been the cause of some criticism of the new Act. Significantly, the draft European Directive on General Product Safety, intended to impose a general safety requirement throughout the European Community, does apply to food.

3.5.1   The Offences
An offence is committed by any person who:

(a) (i)   sells,
     (ii)   offers, exposes or advertises for sale, or
     (iii) has in his possession for sale or for preparation for sale
for human consumption (s. 8(1)(a)), or
(b)   deposits with or consigns to another person for sale or preparation for
sale for human consumption (s. 8(1)(b))

food which fails to comply with a food safety requirement.

Again the presumptions in s. 3, that food commonly used for human consumption is intended for sale for human consumption, apply to reverse the burden of proof in this regard. 'Human consumption' includes uses in the preparation of food for human consumption (s. 53). Thus, for instance, hazelnut puree for use in the manufacture of hazelnut yoghurt would be intended for human consumption as would water used simply to cool cooked food.

It is well established that the offence of selling food unfit for human consumption under previous statutory provisions is an absolute offence, so that it is irrelevant that the seller was unaware of the state of the food (see, e.g., *Hobbs* v *Winchester Corporation* [1901] 2 KB 471). Moreover, there is a long line of authority that where a sale is effected by an employee of a business, the offence is committed by the owner of the business (see, e.g., *Gardner* v *Ackeroyd* [1952] 2 QB 743). This depends on the legal definition of a 'sale' in the Sale of Goods Act 1979 as involving the transfer of property from seller to buyer; hence the seller must be the person who owned the goods prior to the sale, not the agent by whom the sale is effected. Thus if food which contravenes the food safety requirement is sold by an employee at a branch of a chain of supermarkets, the company which owns the chain has committed an offence. On the other hand, there is also authority that the individual employee by whom the transaction is effected can also be convicted (*Preston* v *Albuery* [1964] 2 QB 796).

In the law of sale there is a difference between a sale, under which property passes from buyer to seller at the time the contract is made, and an agreement to sell, under which property passes at some later time. It would seem that a person who delivers food under an agreement to sell could not be convicted of an offence of 'selling' food. However, such arrangements are probably rare in the context of retail sales of food for consumption, and such a seller would, in any case, probably have had the food in his possession for sale, or have offered it or exposed it for sale. Alternatively such a transaction could be regarded as a deposit with or consignment to the consumer for the purposes of the ultimate sale. In the more likely situation where food is delivered by a wholesaler to a retailer pursuant to an agreement to sell there is clearly a deposit or consignment for sale. Thus it has been held that food delivered to agents for retail distribution, although not sold, has been deposited for sale (*Ollett* v *Henry* [1919] 2 KB 88) and even that food carried in a vehicle has been deposited for sale (*Williams* v *Allen* [1916] 1 KB 425).

It has been held that a person can be convicted of an offence involving selling food even though the substance sold is not food at all: what is required is that it should be sold as food. Thus in *Meah* v *Roberts* [1978] 1 All ER 97 the defendant was convicted where he mistakenly supplied the customer with caustic soda instead of lemonade.

The offence in s. 8 extends to a person who advertises food for sale. This is in line with previous law under the 1984 Act s. 1. The advertiser may rely on the defence in s. 22 (see 6.4).

3.5.2   The food safety requirement

The essence of the offence in s. 8 is the sale etc. of food which fails to comply with food safety requirements. Failure to satisfy food safety requirements also underpins the powers of inspection and seizure of food in s. 9. Under s. 8(2), food fails to satisfy food safety requirements in three situations, namely if:—

(a)   It has been rendered injurious to health by any of the operations described in s. 7(1).

(b)   It is unfit for human consumption.

(c)   'It is so contaminated (whether by extraneous matter or otherwise) that it would not be reasonable to expect it to be used for human consumption in that state'.

3.5.3   Part of a batch is unsafe

Section 8(3) is an important new provision. It provides that where any food which fails to comply with food safety requirements is part of a 'batch, lot or consignment', then the whole of that batch, lot or consignment will be presumed not to comply unless the contrary is proved. This is particularly important for the powers of inspection and seizure of food provided by s. 9. 'Batch', 'lot' and 'consignment' are not defined. It was suggested during the Committee stage in the House of Lords that 'batch' refers to similar foods produced at the same time under similar conditions, 'lot' to a 'collection of batches' and 'consignment' to a 'group of products being moved at the same time'. Thus a lorry load of similar products would be part of one consignment.

3.5.4   Acts preparatory to sale

The three elements of the definition of food safety requirements in s. 8(2) are intended to plug perceived gaps in the scope of liability which existed under the 1984 Act. Under the 1984 Act s. 1, it was an offence to sell food which was injurious to health. The new legislation widens liability by extending the offence to include possession for the purposes of preparation for sale and depositing food with or consigning food to another. In addition, the 1984 Act s. 8, made it an offence to sell (etc), possess for sale or preparation for sale, or consign or deposit food which was unfit for human consumption. The offence of sale (etc), possession, deposit or consignment of contaminated food in s. 8 of the new Act is wholly new.

3.5.5   Food injurious to health

It should be noted that s. 8 only applies where the food has been rendered injurious by one of the means described in s. 7 (see 3.4). Thus if food is injurious because of a failure to subject it to a process or treatment, the sale of that food does not constitute an offence under s. 8(2)(a). However, in many cases such food will be unfit for human consumption and thus its sale will be an offence under s. 8(2)(b) above.

3.5.6   Food unfit for human consumption

The concept of unfitness for human consumption is familiar from the existing law. Although 'unfit for human consumption' means more than merely 'unsuitable', food may be unfit for human consumption even though it poses no health hazard. Thus in *David Greig Ltd* v *Goldfinch* (1961) 105 Sol Jo 307 a pork pie was held to be unfit for human consumption when a black mould was found beneath the crust. The mould was actually of the penicillin family and not harmful to humans. Nevertheless, it was held that the justices were entitled to convict the vendor of the pie on the basis that it was unfit for human consumption. On the other hand, previous case law held that the presence of extraneous matter, such as a piece of metal in a cream bun (*J Miller Ltd* v *Battersea BC* [1956] 1 QB 43) or a piece of string in a loaf of bread (*Turner & Son Ltd* v *Owen* [1956] 1 QB 48) did not make food unfit for consumption. Such cases would now be caught, not by para. (b) above, but by the third limb of 'food safety requirements', 'contaminated food' (s. 8(2)(c)). By virtue of s. 8(4) (replacing the provisions in the 1984 Act s. 12), any part of an animal or product derived from an animal slaughtered in a knacker's yard, or whose carcase was brought into a knacker's yard, or, in Scotland, which was slaughtered otherwise than in a slaughterhouse, is automatically deemed unfit for human consumption.

3.5.7   Contaminated food

As noted above, the third head of failure to satisfy 'food safety requirements', where the food is contaminated, is wholly new. It seems that it was intended to cover cases such as *J Miller Ltd* v *Battersea BC* and *Turner & Sons Ltd* v *Owen* (although it has been suggested that such cases could have been prosecuted in the past as cases of selling food not of the nature, substance or quality demanded under s. 2 of the 1984 Act: see the new Act s. 14, chapter 4 below). However, the wording is clearly wider than the decisions in those cases and would appear to cover all types of contamination, including by bacteria, mould or other infection. Many instances of such contamination will also constitute failure to satisfy food safety requirements on other grounds: see, for instance, *David Greig Ltd* v *Goldfinch*.

3.5.8   A General Safety Duty?

Although the 'food safety requirements' established by s. 8 provide a wider basis for criminal liability than existed under the previous law, they do not create such a broad basis for liability in respect of unsafe food as that which applies to other goods by virtue of Part II of the Consumer Protection Act 1987. Section 10 of that Act creates a general safety requirement, and makes it a criminal offence to supply, offer or agree to supply or expose or possess for supply, any goods which are not reasonably safe having regard to all the circumstances. However, food is expressly excluded from the ambit of the 1987 Act. A general safety requirement would plug any loopholes in liability left by the present definition of 'food safety requirements', such as the failure to subject food to a necessary treatment or process mentioned above, and could also be used to meet unforeseen eventualities; it would, for instance, take account of the labelling of food and any instructions supplied with it. However, the Food Safety Act does not create a general safety requirement and so such situations must be covered by specific regulations; problems not covered by such regulations must be dealt with by the power to make emergency control orders under s. 13. However, the European Community has promulgated a draft Directive on General Product Safety which would apply a general safety requirement to products throughout the Community. The draft Directive clearly includes food within its ambit, even though many foods are covered by specific Community requirements. If the draft Directive is adopted in its present form, further legislation will be necessary to ensure UK compliance.

3.5.9   Defences and Penalties

A person charged with an offence under s. 8 may rely on the due diligence defence in s. 21 (see below, chapter 6). The additional defence formerly available (in the 1984 Act s. 8(3)) to a defendant charged with depositing with or consigning to another food unfit for human consumption, that he gave notice to the depositee/consignee that the food was not intended for human consumption, has been repealed. However, a person giving such notice should still escape liability since the giving of such notice would enable him to rebut the presumption that the deposit/consignment was for the purpose of a sale or preparation for sale for human consumption.

A person convicted on indictment of an offence under s. 7 may be sentenced to up to two years' imprisonment and/or a fine. If convicted summarily, the maximum penalty is a £20,000 fine and/or a period of up to six months imprisonment (see s. 35).

3.6   Powers to inspect and seize food

Prosecutions under ss. 7–8 may follow on from routine inspection by enforcement officers, but many are likely to result from complaints from members of the public. Prosecution is thus primarily reactive, and whilst a successful prosecution is likely to have a deterrent effect, additional pre-emptive powers are necessary in order to promote food safety by preventing the sale of unsafe food. A number of such powers are contained in ss. 9–13 of the Act.

Under s. 9 the authorised officer of the enforcement authority has power to inspect food and, if it is unsafe, either to serve a notice preventing its sale for human consumption or removal, or to take the food immediately before a magistrate in order to obtain an order for its destruction. Where a notice is served, the enforcement officer effectively buys time in order to decide if the food in question does satisfy food safety requirements or if it is necessary to seek a destruction order. The powers in s. 9 replace similar powers in the 1984 Act s. 9. However, they differ in a number of details and are wider in one important respect.

3.6.1 Inspection

The enforcement officer may inspect any food intended for human consumption which is sold, offered or exposed for sale or possessed by, deposited with or consigned to any person for the purpose of sale or preparation for sale. The power of inspection may be exercised at any reasonable time (s. 9(1)). The power under s. 9 is only to inspect food: there is no power to inspect premises or processes under this section. The 1984 Act contained a specific power (in s. 11) to examine the contents of any vehicle or container and, where necessary, detain the vehicle or container for that purpose. The power was rarely exercised and there is no equivalent of that provision in the new Act, although the powers in s. 9 would appear to be sufficiently wide to allow examination of vehicle contents.

3.6.1.1 Availability of powers to serve notice and seize food

The officer's powers to serve notices or seize food arise if, on such inspection, the food appears to the officer not to satisfy food safety requirements as defined in s. 8. In addition, by virtue of s. 26(1)(b) regulations made under Part II may provide that food failing to comply with the regulations may be treated as failing to satisfy the food safety requirement for the purposes of s. 9. However, those powers are also available even where there has been no such inspection if it appears to the enforcement officer that any food is likely to cause food poisoning or any disease communicable to human beings (s. 9(2)). There was a similar power under the 1984 Act s. 31, but that only applied where on sampling of the food there were reasonable grounds to suspect that the food was likely to cause food poisoning. Strictly speaking, food poisoning occurs where illness is caused by toxins produced by bacteria in the food consumed. Many instances of what is colloquially known as 'food poisoning' are actually cases of food borne infection where bacteria in food enter the body when food is consumed and bacteria multiply inside the body. The Act does not define 'food poisoning', but under the old law, the expression was interpreted widely to cover illness of both chemical and biological origin. Even if it is argued that food-borne infections are not food poisoning, they are likely to be held to fall within the reference to 'disease communicable to human beings'. That reference would also include other diseases: for instance if evidence were to show that BSE can be transmitted to human beings from infected foodstuffs, the s. 9 powers would be available in respect of food containing the organism responsible for BSE.

Nevertheless, s. 9(2) may cause difficulties. The powers to serve notices and seize food are available where 'it appears . . . that any food is likely to cause food poisoning . . .'. Environmental health officers exercising the s. 9 powers should be able, by virtue of their training, to recognise when food is likely to cause food poisoning. However, an implementation advisory committee on the enforcement of the Act is to be set up and that committee may issue guidance on the meaning of food poisoning as part of a code of practice on the implementation of s. 9. It should also be noted that s. 40 of the Act contains power for the Minister to issue codes of practice to give guidance on the enforcement of the Act.

The powers in s. 9 are available where it appears to the enforcement officer that food fails to satisfy food safety requirements, or is likely to cause food poisoning or a communicable disease. There is no need for the officer to have reasonable grounds for his belief. In practice an enforcement officer is most unlikely to seek to exercise the powers under s. 9 in the absence of reasonable grounds. Where food is seized, it must be taken before a magistrate for an order for its destruction. The person from whom the food is seized has a right to be heard on that application. If no order is made, or if a notice under s. 9 is withdrawn, compensation is payable to the owner of the food (s. 9(7)).

3.6.1.2 Powers under section 9   Section 9 gives the enforcement officer the power either to serve notice restricting the movement or sale of food, or to seize it immediately.

A notice under s. 9(3) may notify the person in charge of the food that the food or a specified part of it is not to be used for human consumption and is not to be removed, unless it be to some place specified in the notice. It is a criminal offence, punishable by a fine and/or imprisonment (s. 35(2)), knowingly to contravene the requirements of such a notice (s. 9(3)). In the general criminal law, an offence is commited 'knowingly' if the accused has knowledge of all the elements of the offence; thus in this context the offence would require the accused to know of the order and that his actions contravened it. However, an accused who deliberately shuts his eyes to obvious facts or to a means of discovering them will be treated as knowing them.

The service of a notice under s. 9 gives the enforcement officer time to decide if the food satisfies food safety requirements; if satisfied that the food does comply with food safety requirements, the officer must withdraw the notice (s. 9(4)(a)); compensation is then payable in respect of any depreciation in the value of the food (s. 9(7)). If the officer is not satisfied that the food complies with food safety requirements, he may seize the food in order to have it dealt with by a magistrate. The officer must make his decision as soon as is reasonably practicable and in any event within 21 days. During that time the food is likely to be subjected to analysis and tests using the powers under ss. 29–30.

Where food is seized, either:

(a)   following inspection (s. 9(1)),
(b)   where it appears likely to cause food poisoning etc (s. 9(2)) or
(c)   following service of a notice (s. 9(4)),

the officer must notify the person in charge of the food of his intention to have it dealt with by a magistrate. Any person who might be liable to prosecution for an offence under ss. 7 or 8 of the Act in respect of that food may then appear before the magistrate and be heard and call witnesses ((s 9(5)); at such hearing he might explain that it was intended that the food should undergo further processing to make it safe. The magistrate may hear 'such evidence as he considers appropriate in the circumstances'. If he decides that the food fails to comply with food safety requirements, he must condemn the food and order it to be disposed of so as to prevent its use for human consumption; in that case he must order that any expenses reasonably incurred in connection with the destruction of the food be defrayed by the owner of the food (s. 9(6)). Where food which fails to comply with food safety requirements forms part of a lot, batch or consignment, the presumption in s. 8(3) applies, and the whole of the relevant lot, batch or consignment is presumed not to comply. Thus a destruction order could apply to the whole lot, batch or consignment. However, if the magistrate refuses to condemn the food, compensation is payable to the owner in respect of any depreciation in its value (s. 9(7)).

3.6.2 Compensation

Section 9(7) attempts to protect the owner of the food against unjustified interference by requiring the food authority to compensate the owner of food for any depreciation in its value where either a notice under s. 9(3) is withdrawn, or where a magistrate refuses a destruction order under s. 9(6). In the event of any dispute, the amount of compensation payable is to be fixed by arbitration (s. 9(8)). Unlike the 1984 Act (ss. 108–9), the new Act does not stipulate how the arbitration is to be established or conducted. Arbitration under s. 9(8) will therefore be governed by the Arbitration Acts (see Arbitration Act 1950, s. 31) and will be by reference to a single arbitrator; the identity of the arbitrator should be agreed by the parties, but in the event of a failure to agree there may be an application to the High Court to appoint an arbitrator. Moreover, the compensation payable is limited to 'any depreciation in [the] value [of the food in question] resulting from the action taken by the authorised officer'. Thus compensation will not be available for profits lost due to the seizure of the food, nor due to the adverse effect on trade and goodwill of the service of a s. 9 notice. It is unlikely that compensation will be available through any other legal mechanism. An individual officer may not be held personally liable in respect of any act done in the course of his employment in the performance or purported performance of his duties under the Act, provided he acted in good faith (s. 44). Of course, compensation may be recoverable if it can be shown that an officer acted maliciously, but that is rarely likely to be the case. It might be easier to establish negligence in the exercise of the statutory powers. A food authority remains liable in respect of acts done by its officers, even in good faith (s. 44(2)), and thus would be vicariously liable for negligent acts of such officers. However, in light of recent developments in the law of negligence, the importance of food safety, the nature of the powers exercised by enforcement officers and the availability of statutory compensation, it is unlikely that a duty of care would be held to exist in relation to the service of notices or seizure of food under s. 9, even if negligence could be proved. Thus it would seem that in the event of unjustified notices or seizures, many commercial losses are likely to go uncompensated.

3.7   Improvement notices

Whereas the powers in s. 9 are exercisable only in respect of unsafe food, ss. 10–12 contain further powers of enforcement available in a wide range of circumstances. They replace powers contained in the 1984 Act, ss. 13–15 and 21–26.

Section 10 allows enforcement officers to ensure compliance with regulations concerned with food safety and hygiene made under s. 16. It has no direct equivalent in the earlier legislation. Where an authorised officer has reasonable grounds to believe that the proprietor of a food business is not complying with regulations which require, prohibit or regulate the use of any process or treatment in the preparation of food (s. 10(3)(a): see s. 16(1)(c)) or which provide for the observance of hygienic conditions and practices in connection with the carrying out of commercial operations with respect to food or food sources (s. 10(3)(b): see s. 16(1)(d)), the officer may serve an improvement notice.

Such a notice must:—

(a)   State the grounds for believing that the proprietor is not complying with regulations.

(b)   Specify the matters which constitute non-compliance.

(c)   Specify measures which, in the enforcement officer's opinion, the proprietor must take to ensure compliance.

(d)   Specify a time limit for those measures, or measures at least equivalent, to be taken; the specified time limit must not be less than 14 days.

(e)   Indicate the right to appeal against an improvement notice, and the time limit for making such appeal.

The aim of the section is clearly to raise standards. It is an offence to fail to comply with an improvement notice, punishable with a fine and/or imprisonment (s. 35). Any person aggrieved by the service of an improvement notice may appeal to a magistrates' court within the period specified in the notice for improvement, or within one month of service of the notice, whichever is the shorter (s. 37). A further appeal may be made to the Crown Court (s. 38). Once an appeal is lodged, the period for compliance with the improvement notice is effectively suspended (s. 39(2), (3)). On an appeal, a court has extensive powers to cancel or confirm the notice, including power to confirm it subject to modifications (s. 39(1)).

Section 10 has a wide application. An improvement notice can be served on the proprietor of any food business. The 'proprietor' is the person by whom a food business (see 2.3.3) is carried on (s. 53(1)). Thus any business concerned with the sale (etc), advertisement, delivery, serving, preparation, wrapping, labelling, storage, transport, import or export of food may be the subject of an improvement notice. Further, as the definition of food business includes 'food sources' businesses dealing with growing crops and/or livestock are potentially within the ambit of s. 10. However, the only regulations concerned with food sources in connection with which an improvement notice can be served are those concerned with securing the observance of hygienic conditions and practices. It would seem that an improvement notice could be served on a slaughterhouse, a farm dairy or on a poultry farm selling live birds for slaughter on the premises.

3.8 Prohibition orders

Section 11 makes further powers available in the event of contravention of food process or hygiene regulations. Under that section, if the proprietor of a food business is convicted of an offence under those regulations, the court has power in certain circumstances to make orders prohibiting the use of a specified process or treatment, or of premises or equipment, for the purposes of a food business, and even to prohibit the involvement of the convicted proprietor in the management of a food business. This is considerably wider than the equivalent powers in the 1984 Act, which allowed the court in similar circumstances to make limited orders closing or restricting the use of premises. The intention is to prevent a convicted proprietor having one set of premises closed down, only to re-open in new premises almost immediately.

3.8.1 Conditions for making an order
For the power to make a prohibition order under s. 11 to arise, two conditions must be fulfilled:

(a) The proprietor of the food business must be convicted of an offence under regulations which require, prohibit or regulate the use of any process or treatment in the preparation of food or which provide for the observance of hygienic conditions and practices in connection with the carrying out of commercial operations with respect to food or food sources: i.e. the same class of regulations which give rise to the power to serve improvement notices under s. 10. It is likely that in most cases, contravention of regulations will be dealt with in the first instance by an improvement notice, with prosecution being undertaken either where such notice fails to lead to the desired improvement or where the contravention is particularly serious. In all probability, most prosecutions leading to prohibition orders will be for contravention of hygiene regulations.

(b) The court which convicts the proprietor must be satisfied that the 'health risk condition' is fulfilled in relation to the relevant food business. The health risk condition is fulfilled if there is risk of injury to health (as defined in s. 7) due to:

(i) The use of any process or treatment for the purposes of the business.

(ii) The construction of any premises used for the purposes of the business; it would seem that 'construction' refers to the design and method of construction rather than the act of constructing premises; 'premises' is defined in s. 1 to include any place, vehicle, stall or moveable structure.

(iii) The use of any equipment (defined to include 'any apparatus': s. 53) for the purposes of the business.

(iv) The state or condition of any premises or equipment used for the purposes of the business (s. 11(2)).

3.8.2 Nature of prohibition
If the two conditions are fulfilled, the court must impose 'the appropriate prohibition', depending on the nature of the health risk (s. 11(3)). The court

also has a discretion to make a further order prohibiting the involvement of the convicted proprietor in the management of a food business (s. 11(4)).

The nature of the mandatory prohibition depends on the manner in which the health risk condition is fulfilled. In cases falling under para. (a) above, the court must prohibit the use of the process or treatment in question for the purposes of the particular business. In cases falling under para. (b) or (c), the court must prohibit the use of the premises or equipment for the purposes of the particular business or for the purposes of a food business 'of the same class or description'. For instance, where premises are used as a take away fish and chip shop, an order might prohibit their use for any type of food business, or for use as a fish and chip shop or other cooked fast food take away. In cases falling under para. (d) the court must prohibit the use of the equipment or premises for the purposes of any food business.

Such an order must be served on the proprietor of the business as soon as practicable after it is made, and a copy must be affixed in a conspicuous position on any premises used for the purposes of the business as are thought appropriate. It is an offence knowingly to contravene such an order (s. 11(5)), punishable in accordance with s. 35. A person who removes or defaces such an order will be guilty of an offence, either under the Criminal Damage Act 1971, or under the Magistrates Courts Act 1980 s. 63, where an order has been made under that section prohibiting the removal or defacing of the notice.

The prohibition order remains in force until the enforcement authority issues a certificate indicating that it is satisfied that the proprietor of the business has taken sufficient steps to remove the relevant health risk (s. 11(6)(a)). Whilst a prohibition order remains in force, a food business may be unable to trade. It is therefore necessary that such orders be lifted speedily where the relevant health risk has been removed. The Act therefore provides that a certificate lifting a prohibition order must be issued within three days of the authority being satisfied that the health risk has been abated (s. 11(7)). The proprietor may apply for such a certificate: in that case the authority must reach its decision to issue a certificate as soon as is reasonably practicable and, in any event, within 14 days (s. 11(7)(a)). If a certificate is refused, the authority must give notice to the proprietor of the reasons for the refusal (s. 11(7)(b)) and of the right to appeal to a magistrates' court against the refusal. The proprietor may, within one month, appeal against refusal of a certificate (s. 37).

Additionally, where the proprietor of a food business is convicted of an offence under hygiene regulations, then if the court thinks it proper in all the circumstances, it may impose an order on the proprietor personally, prohibiting his participation in the management of any food business, or in any food business of a specified class or description (s. 11(4)). This personal prohibition order differs in several respects from orders relating to premises, processes and equipment. First, the power to make such an order is only available on a conviction under hygiene regulations; second, there is no need for a health risk condition to be fulfilled; third, the court has a discretion to make such an order whereas other types of prohibition are mandatory where the appropriate conditions are fulfilled. The Act recognises that the proprietor of a business may not be personally responsible for the day to day management of an individual business or outlet: there is therefore further power (s. 11(10)) to make such a prohibition order in respect of the 'manager of a food business', defined as 'any person who is entrusted by the proprietor with the day to day running of the business' (s. 11(11)). This power may be particularly important, not only in enabling a prohibition order to be directed against the real culprit, but also where a business has a number of outlets (for instance, a chain of supermarkets), where a prohibition order against the proprietor would close down the whole business with drastic effects on employment and consumer choice. A prohibition order is only likely to be made againt the proprietor of such a multi-outlet business where there are breaches of hygiene regulations at a number of branches, or where a breach can be shown to be due to general company policy.

Personal prohibition orders may give rise to some difficult questions of interpretation. 'Manager' is defined only for the purposes of s. 11(10) and 'management' not defined at all. If an order was made against the proprietor of a small bakery, would that pevent him working as 'manager' of the in-store bakery department at a branch of a supermarket chain? The answer might well depend on the actual degree of control over the bakery given to the departmental manager in the individual organisation, and thus might differ from one organisation to another.

An order againt a proprietor or manager must be served on the person against whom it is made. Such an order only ceases to have effect on the court giving a direction to that effect (s. 11(6)(b)). The person subject to prohibition must apply to the court for such a direction, when the court will consider all the circumstances of the case, including the conduct of the applicant since the order was made. However, the court may not entertain an application made within six months of the original prohibition or within three months of a previous failed application (s. 11(8)). A personal prohibition order must therefore remain in force for at least six months and it is likely to be an important and powerful weapon in the enforcement of hygiene standards. It is a criminal offence for a person subject to a prohibition knowingly to be involved in a food business in contravention of the order whilst it remains in force (s. 11(5)).

3.9 Emergency orders

The power to make prohibition orders under s. 11 may be a valuable weapon in support of public health and consumer safety, in particular in preventing repetition of unsafe or unhygienic practices. However, an order under s. 11 can only be made after a person has been convicted of an offence under the appropriate regulations. Clearly there may be situations where there is such an immediate risk to public health that action must be taken urgently, without the delay which a prosecution might entail. Sections 12–13 contain powers allowing such urgent or emergency action to be taken. Section 12 allows an authorised officer of an enforcement authority to take urgent action against an individual food business proprietor by serving emergency prohibition notices or applying to the court for emergency prohibition orders, whilst s. 13 allows the Minister to take emergency action affecting a range of businesses or a whole class of businesses where there is a more widespread, immediate risk to health.

The powers in s. 12 replace powers to take emergency action formerly contained in the 1984 Act, s. 22. Those powers were considerably more restricted than the new provisions, since they only allowed an emergency order to be made by a court on three days' notice, and then in relation only to premises or their use. The new s. 12 allows the enforcement authority to take immediate action without a court order, permitting a speedier and more flexible response, and also allows a wider range of orders to be made.

3.9.1   Emergency prohibition notices

An authorised officer of an enforcement authority has power to serve an emergency prohibition notice ('epn') if the health risk condition is satisfied. 'Health risk condition' is defined in the same way as in s. 11(2), except that for the purposes of s. 12 there must be an imminent risk of injury to health (s. 12(4)). Where the health risk condition is satisfied, the authorised officer is empowered to serve an 'epn' containing the 'appropriate prohibition', as defined in s. 11(3). Thus the full range of prohibitions discussed above, relating to premises, equipment or processes, is available on an emergency basis. Once an 'epn' is made, the enforcement authority must, as soon as reasonably practicable, affix a copy of the notice to a conspicuous part of such premises used for the business as it thinks appropriate, and it is then a criminal offence, punishable in accordance with s. 35, for any person knowingly to contravene the prohibition (s. 12(5)).

The power to serve an 'epn' without the need to obtain a court order or bring a prosecution is clearly an important addition to the powers of the enforcement authority. However, it is also a potentially draconian power, and it is necessary to strike a balance between the public health interest and the interests of the business affected by the 'epn'. The Act seeks to strike that balance by severely restricting the duration of an 'epn' and providing that such a prohibition will remain in force for a short time unless application is made to a court for an emeregency prohibition order ('epo'), and providing for compensation to be payable where an 'epn' is served without proper grounds. Thus, unless an application is made to the court for an 'epo' within three days of the serving of an 'epn', the 'epn' will cease to have effect (s. 12(7)(a)). Moreover, in that case the enforcement authority is obliged to compensate the proprietor of the business on whom the notice was served in respect of any loss suffered by reason of complying with the notice (s. 12(10)). If an application for an 'epo' is made, the 'epn' remains in force until that application is determined or abandoned (s. 12(7)(b)). If at the hearing of that application no order is made, compensation will be payable to the proprietor of the business on which the 'epn' was served, unless the court declares itself satisfied that the health risk condition was fulfilled at the time the 'epn' was served. This is important where the original notice was justified but the business affected takes steps to remedy the position before the hearing of the 'epo' application.

Alternatively, a notice will cease to have effect if the enforcement authority issues a certificate indicating that it is satisfied that sufficient measures have been taken by the proprietor to ensure that the health risk condition is no longer fulfilled (s. 12(8)). The proprietor of the business may apply for such a certificate at any time after an 'epn' is served, and the enforcement authority must then decide as soon as reasonably practicable, and in any event within 14 days, whether or not to issue a certificate. Once the authority is satisfied that the risk to health has been removed, it must issue the relevant certificate within three days (s. 12(9)). If the authority is not satisfied, it must give notice to the proprietor indicating the reasons for refusing the certificate (s. 12(9)(b)). The proprietor may appeal to a magistrates' court against the refusal of a certificate within one month of the refusal (s. 37) and the notice of refusal must give notice of this right to appeal. However, such an appeal is to be made by complaint to a magistrates' court. In the case of a refusal to lift an 'epn', there will generally be an application by the enforcement authority for an 'epo' already pending; it will probably be better for the proprietor to contest the making of such an order in those proceedings, since that application is likely to be heard before any appeal against the refusal of a certificate. In any case where compensation is payable under s. 12(10), any dispute as to the amount of compensation payable is to be settled by arbitration.

3.9.2 Emergency prohibition orders

An 'epo' is made by a magistrates' court on application by an authorised officer of an enforcement authority (s. 12(2)); such an application can only be made if the officer has given notice of his intention to apply for the order to the proprietor of the business in question at least one day before the application (s. 12(3)). Presumably enforcement authorities will normally proceed initially by serving an 'epn' and will give notice of intention to apply for an 'epo' at the same time.

The court has power to make an 'epo' if it is satisfied on such an application that the health risk condition is fulfilled in relation to the business. As in the case of an 'epn', this has the same meanning as in s. 11(2), save that for an emergency order there must be an imminent risk of injury to health (s. 12(4)). The order will impose the 'appropriate prohibition', defined as in s. 11(3). It should be noted that there is no power under s. 12 to make an 'epo', equivalent to an order under s. 11(4), in relation to the proprietor or manager of a business. Where an 'epo' is made in respect of a food business, s. 11(1) applies as if the proprietor of the food business in question has been convicted of an offence under regulations to which s. 11 applies (s. 11(9)); however, this does not appear to be sufficient to allow an order to be made under s. 11(4). If an 'epo' is made, a copy must be served on the proprietor of the business and a further copy affixed to premises used for the purposes of the business as soon as possible, and it is an offence knowingly to contravene an 'epo' (s. 12(6)).

It should be noted that under both s. 11 and s. 12, copies of notices and orders must be affixed in a conspicuous place on such premises used for the purposes of the business as the enforcement authority considers appropriate. In the case of a multi-outlet business, this will presumably be the particular outlet affected. However, there appears to be nothing to require the notice to be so affixed, nor to restrict enforcement officers to one single notice. Clearly, if the offending outlet is not the subject of a notice, it might be difficult to prosecute for contravention of the notice/order, but if several outlets could be 'noticed', there might be a serious impact on the trade of the business in question. Provided the authority acts in good faith there seems nothing to prevent this, unless administrative law remedies would be available to the business affected.

An 'epo' remains in force, like an 'epn', until the issue of a certificate by the enforcement authority indicating satisfaction that the health risk condition is no longer fulfilled (s. 12(8)). The procedure for applying for and issuing such a certificate is the same as that in the case of an 'epn'; however, in the event of a refusal of a certificate, any appeal to the court will have to be by a separate complaint to the court since, ex hypothesi, there will no longer be any proceedings pending.

3.9.3   *Emergency control orders*

Section 12 gives the local authority power to take emergency measures to deal with specific health risks caused by individual businesses. However, as several of the well publicised incidents of recent years have demonstrated, many health hazards posed by food are much more widespread and require urgent, cohesive measures to be taken in more than one area. Accordingly s. 13 contains powers to deal with such widespread emergencies, allowing the Minister to make emergency control orders ('eco's). An 'eco' may prohibit the carrying out of any commercial operations with respect to any food, food sources or contact materials which appear to the Minister to involve an imminent risk of injury to health (s. 13(1)); contravention of an 'eco' is a criminal offence (s. 13(2)), punishable in accordance with s. 35. The Minister has power to abrogate an 'eco', either absolutely or conditionally, in individual cases (s. 13(3)) and such Ministerial consent provides a defence to a charge of contravening an 'eco' (s. 13(4)). Section 13(5) gives the Minister further powers to give such directions or take such actions as appear to him to be necessary or expedient to prevent the carrying out of commercial operations with respect to any food, food source or contact material which he believes to be covered by an 'eco'. This is clearly a wide power; but whilst the Minister has an unfettered discretion in relation to the decision to issue directions or take other steps, which might include the impounding, seizure or destruction of goods, he must have reasonable grounds for his belief that the food etc in respect of which such directions or steps are taken is covered by the 'eco'. Failure to comply with a direction under s. 13(5) is a criminal offence (s. 13(6)) and in addition, where any person's failure to comply with an 'eco' or a direction under s. 13(5) causes the Minister to take action, he may recover from that person any expenses incurred in taking that action (s. 13(7)). In light of the provisions of s. 13(6)–(7), a person affected by an 'eco' or related direction will normally be advised to comply in order to avoid further financial liability. There is no provision for compensation if an 'eco' is made in error, despite an attempt to introduce such a provision in the House of Lords, and the only protection available to food businesses against such an error is likely to be insurance.

Chapter Four
Consumer Protection

4.1 Introduction

The offences considered in this chapter fall under the general title of consumer protection measures. They seek to prevent consumers from being misled and to ensure they receive food of the appropriate nature, substance and quality. Food Safety Act 1990 s. 14 makes it an offence to sell food not of the nature or substance or quality demanded. Similar offences are created in relation to drugs by the Medicines Act 1968 and for animal feeding stuffs by the Agriculture Act 1970. Section 15 makes it an offence to falsely or misleadingly describe, advertise or present food. It should also be borne in mind that food is also subject to the Labelling of Food Regulations 1984, SI 1984/1305. Without discussing the detail of the Regulations it should be noted that they contain a prohibition on the misleading presentation of food, including its shape, appearance or packing and the way it is arranged. The Regulations also prescribe, subject to certain exceptions, the information that must be given with the food. This includes a list of ingredients, an indication of minimum durability, any special storage conditions or conditions of use and the name and address of the manufacturer, packer or seller. They also, inter alia, impose conditions on the use of claims, for example about the food's protein or cholesterol content and require that, if emphasis is placed on the presence or low content of an ingredient, the maximum or minimum percentage of the ingredient should be stated.

4.2 Nature, substance and quality

The 1990 Act s. 14 substantially reproduces the Food Act 1984, s. 2 making it an offence for any person to sell to the purchaser's prejudice any food which is not of the nature or substance or quality demanded by the purchaser.

4.2.1 'Any person'
The offence must be committed by a person. The Interpretation Act 1978, s. 5 and sch. 1, provides that, unless the contrary intention appears, 'person' is to

be construed as including a body of persons corporate or unincorporate. Often the offence will be committed by a junior employee. As the offence is an absolute one, that person could be prosecuted but in practice the authorities will prefer to prosecute someone more senior. A difficult question then arises as to whether the manager of the establishment or the business itself should be liable. *Goodfellow* v *Johnson* [1966] 1 QB 83 concerned a barmaid who served gin containing too much water. Liability was imposed on the licensee rather than the brewery since Lord Parker CJ argued that the case turned not on 'the parting of the title by the owner' but rather on the 'physical handling and handing over of the goods by way of sale'. This could only be done by the licensee. With respect it is submitted that this should be limited to the unique position of a licensee under the Licensing Acts. If extended further it would effectively remove liability from businesses. Indeed in *Booth* v *Helliwell* [1914] 3 KB 252 the company was held liable because the shop assistant was held to be the servant of the company and not of the shop's general manager. A person has been held responsible for his employee's acts even where he has expressly forbidden the employee to adulterate food and has taken precautions to prevent him from doing so (*Brown* v *Foot* (1892) 56 JP 581, *Andrews* v *Luckin* (1917) 117 LT 726). The employer may not be liable, however, if the employee acted outside the scope of his authority (*Whittaker* v *Forshaw* [1919] 2 KB 419), although even a limited authority to sell may cause liability to be imposed (*Elder* v *Bishop Auckland Co-operative Society* (1917) 86 LJKB 1412).

4.2.2 'Who sells'
The offence requires a sale although it will be remembered that s. 2 gives sale an extended meaning to include food which is supplied in the course of a business or offered as a prize (see 2.4). For the offence under consideration to be committed the sale must be a sale for human consumption (s. 14(2)). No offence under this section, would, for example, be committed in a sale of animal feed. The offence does not extend to 'offers' for sale, presumably because of the need for a demand from a purchaser against which to judge the expected nature, substance or quality of the food. However this would seem to leave a loophole whereby a retailer could escape conviction by refusing to serve someone he believed to be an enforcement officer. This is however not likely to be a sensible long-term tactic.

4.2.3 'Any food'
Food is defined by s. 1 of the 1990 Act (see 2.1). Moreover it was held in *Meah* v *Roberts* [1978] 1 All ER 97 that the expression 'sells any food' means 'sells something as a food'. That case involved a prosecution for the sale of caustic soda which by accident was supplied instead of the lemonade ordered.

4.2.4 'To the purchaser's prejudice' and 'demanded by the purchaser'
These two phrases are to some extent inter-dependent since whether a purchaser is prejudiced by the nature, substance or quality of the food will depend upon what the purchaser demanded.

The statute explicitly states that there can be no defence that the purchaser was not prejudiced, simply because the food was bought for analysis or examination (s. 14(2)). Similarly it has been held that a purchaser can be prejudiced even if the food was bought on his behalf by another. Thus food does not have to be bought by the inspector personally, but can be bought by a more junior employee (*Garforth* v *Esam* (1892) 56 JP 521). The purchaser prejudiced is taken to be the ordinary purchaser. It is irrelevant that the purchaser may have special knowledge (other than from information supplied by the seller) that the article was not of the nature, substance or quality demanded. Equally it is important to remember that the nature, substance or quality of the product should be judged in relation to the demand made by the purchaser. The demand identifies the product and grade or type of product demanded. Thus in *McDonald's Hamburgers* v *Windle* [1987] Crim LR 200 a request for 'Diet McDonald's Cola' caused an offence to be committed when ordinary Cola was served. The standard demanded is to be judged in the light of what the purchaser expected to receive. The evidence of a public analyst is not necessarily conclusive. So in *Collins Arden Products Ltd* v *Barking Borough* [1943] KB 419 no offence was committed when cordial was supplied containing saccharin. The evidence of the public analysts disagreed over whether the term cordial in relation to a non-alcoholic drink implied that it contained sugar to give it a heartening effect. The Court held that, notwithstanding the expert opinion, the appropriate test was the view of the ordinary purchaser. Even if there is no statutory or regulatory standard, evidence of what standard a public analyst would expect is not a conclusive answer to the question of what the purchaser demanded. In *Goldup* v *John Manson* [1982] QB 161 a public analyst gave evidence that the fat content of minced beef should not exceed 25 per cent. Nevertheless a butcher escaped conviction when he sold mince beef with a fat content in excess of this figure. It was relevant that the shop sold two types of minced beef; the one in question was cheaper but had a higher fat content. It was for the prosecution to prove that when buying the lower price mince, the puchaser demanded mince with less fat content than the 33 per cent which it actually contained.

It is clear that the puchaser's demands are affected by the information supplied to him. Thus in the *McDonald's* case the purchaser expected the Cola to conform to the Nutrition Guide displayed on the premises. More difficult to answer is whether any potential prejudice can be countered by a notice drawing the deficiency to the purchaser's attention. The judiciary have taken a robust view of such notices and in the Scottish case of *Brander* v *Kinnear* (1923) SC (J) 42 it was said that to be effective the notice must be both clear and unambiguous and acquaint the purchaser not only with the fact, but also with the character of the prejudice they are being asked to accept. This view was endorsed south of the border in *Rodburn* v *Hudson* [1925] 1 KB 225.

A purchaser will clearly be prejudiced if the food has been adulterated. However food does not have to endanger a purchaser's health for him to be prejudiced. Prejudice is suffered if a purchaser receives food inferior to that which he demanded and paid for.

4.2.5 *'Nature or substance or quality'*
The three central concepts of nature, substance or quality are used disjunctively and so the prosecuting authority must state which of the three possible

offences the defendant is charged with. (Care must be taken with early cases on these words as the Sale of Food and Drugs Act 1875, s. 6 drafted this phrase conjunctively. This was changed to its present form by the Food and Drugs (Amendment) Act 1928). This is illustrated by *Bastin* v *Davies* [1950] 1 All ER 1095 where an information (a document by which the Crown commences legal proceedings) alleging some beef sausages were 'not of the nature or not of the substance or not of the quality demanded' was held bad for duplicity. The Court held that the defendant was entitled to be told of what he was being charged. However the prosecutor was advised that if he was unsure of which head the offence fell under he should issue two or more informations. Thus it would be possible to charge someone with selling food not of the nature and not of the substance and not of the quality demanded so long as the charges appeared on three separate informations. This would also appear to be the position under the Magistrates' Courts Rules 1981 (SI 1981/552). While r. 12(1) prohibits trials on informations charging more than one offence, the same document can contain two or more informations (r. 12(2)).

It will be apparent from the discussion which follows that there is a degree of overlap between the terms nature, substance and quality. Where this is the case the prosecutor can choose whichever he considers to be the most appropriate. For example, where white fish was used instead of scampi it is likely that the food was not of the nature as well as not of the substance demanded, but this did not invalidate an information which simply alleged that it was not of the substance demanded (*Preston* v *Greenclose* (1975) 139 JP 245).

4.2.6 'Nature'
Food will not be of the nature demanded even if it is pure and unadulterated so long as it is different from the food demanded. Thus an offence was committed when the abortifacient 'Savin' was supplied instead of the drug 'Saffron' (*Knight* v *Bowers* (1885) 14 QBD 845 — when that case was decided drugs were covered by the same provision). Similarly it was an offence in *Meah* v *Roberts* [1978] 1 All ER 97 to supply caustic soda instead of lemonade. It would be an offence to supply margarine instead of butter, chicory instead of coffee or cod instead of haddock. The Courts will imply what they believe the ordinary purchaser would expect the nature of the food to be. Thus in *Riley Bros (Halifax) Ltd* v *Hallimond* (1927) 44 TLR 238 a conviction was upheld against a confectioner who sold 'butter toffee' which in fact also contained coconut fat. The description 'butter toffee' was found to imply that no fat except butter was used in its manufacture.

4.2.7 'Substance'
In *Few* v *Robinson* [1921] 3 KB 504 milk was found not to offend against this section so long as it came from a cow even if its fat content did not meet the statutory requirement. This decision seems wrong and the Court seems to have erred in believing the section was limited to cases of adulteration. However for a complaint of this nature it is better to charge the seller under the quality head rather than alleging that the food was not of the substance demanded.

Food will be of the substance demanded if it satisfies the generic definition given to a type of food. In *Anderson v Britcher* (1914) 110 LT 335 sugar was sold as 'Demerara Sugar' although it had been grown in Mauritius and not Demerara. No offence was said to be committed as 'Demerara Sugar' referred to a type of sugar and not a place of origin. It was significant that the sugar actually sold was of the same value as sugar from Demerara. If the place of origin affects the quality of the product e.g. Welsh butter or German beer, then an offence may be committed if food from elsewhere is sold under that description.

The presence of a foreign substance in the food will render it not of the substance demanded. For example, a cake would not be of the substance demanded if it contained glass. Similarly an offence is possibly committed if pesticide residues are found on crops. In *Hall v Owen-Jones and Jones* [1967] 3 All ER 209 milk containing penicillin was found to be not of the substance demanded.

When there are prescribed statutory or regulatory standards, food must comply with these standards in order to be of the substance demanded. Thus, for example, the Food Standards (Fish Cakes) Order 1950 (discussed below), required fish cakes to have a 35 per cent minimum fish content. A food described as a 'fish cake' containing a lower percentage would not be of the substance demanded. In this respect *(Thomas) Robinson Sons & Co Ltd v Allardice* (1944) 170 LT 297 is anomalous as the statutory standard was held to be inapplicable. This case can however be explained because the food was actually supplied before the relevant order was made and the order was not made for reasons of consumer protection but rather for economic reasons due to the impending war.

Where there is a prescribed standard then the food should prima facie comply with that standard (*Dickins v Randerson* [1901] 1 KB 437), although evidence can be adduced to show that there is a lower acceptable commercial standard (*Boots Cash Chemists (Southern) Ltd v Cowling* (1903) 38 LT 539). In the absence of a fixed standard it is for the court to decide the appropriate standard. This is a question of fact, which explains why a conviction for selling minced beef containing 32.7 per cent fat content could be upheld in *TW Lawrence & Sons Ltd v Burleigh* (1982) 80 LGR 631, while in *Goldup v John Manson* minced beef containing 33 per cent fat was not found to contravene the provision. In determining the appropriate standard the Court can have regard to expert evidence by a public analyst but should not be slavishly bound by it and price may be a relevant factor (*Goldup v John Manson*). It is not necessary to show that there is a fixed standard for a food so long as it can be shown that the food fell below the minimum standard possible. Thus in *Tonkin v Victor Value Ltd* [1962] 1 All ER 821 it was adequate to show that a 'mock salmon cutlette' should have at least 35 per cent fish, the minimum fish content which had been prescribed for fish cakes by the Food Standards (Fish Cakes) Order 1950.

4.2.8 'Quality'
Reference to 'quality' does not simply refer to description but also to the commercial quality of the food (*Anness v Grivell* [1915] 3 KB 685). Thus, for

example, if a customer asks for a 'scotch' it may not be sufficient to give him a whisky from Scotland if the circumstances lead him to expect a malt whisky. The quality to be expected depends upon all the circumstances including such matters as the price and any express contractual terms. A cheap price could indicate an expectation of below average quality, but it is submitted that all food must satisfy the conditions of merchantable quality and fitness for purpose if a conviction is to be avoided. However it should be borne in mind that the definition of merchantable quality, in the Sale of Goods Act 1979, s. 14(6), is similarly flexible taking account of price and other factors.

If a product is not perfectly constituted, for example milk containing less fat than would be expected, the correct charge is that the food is not of the quality demanded. The quality will be inadequate if a foreign body is in the food, for example the house-fly in the milk bottle in *Newton* v *West Vale Creamery Co* (1956) 120 JP 318 or the nail in the bag of sweets in *Lindley* v *George W Horner & Co Ltd* [1950] 1 All ER 234. Extraneous matter will affect the quality of food if its presence is deleterious, but equally the quality of the food will be affected if a purchaser could reasonably object to the extraneous matter being present. Thus an offence was committed in *Barber* v *Co-operative Wholesale Society Ltd* (1983) 81 LGR 762 when a green plastic straw was found inside a milk bottle despite the lack of evidence that the straw was not sterile.

4.3   Falsely describing advertising and presenting food

The Food Safety Act 1990, s. 15 makes it an offence to falsely describe, advertise or present food. This is partially a re-enactment of the Food Act 1984, s. 7 but the offence of falsely presenting food is new.

4.3.1   Falsely describing food
The first offence which s. 15 provides for is that of selling, offering or exposing for sale, or possessing for the purposes of sale, food which has a label either falsely describing the food or which is likely to mislead as to the nature or substance or quality of the food (s. 15(1)). The offence therefore requires the person charged either to have sold the food or to have offered or exposed it for sale. The extended definition of sale, which the Food Safety Act 1990 applies, has already been discussed (see 2.4). For the purposes of this section, however, references to 'sale' mean sales for human consumption (s. 15(5)). The definitions of 'food' and 'human consumption' have already been discussed (see 2.1 and 2.5).

4.3.1.1   'Label'   The offence requires there to have been a label either given away with the food or displayed with any food offered or exposed for sale or in the defendant's possession for the purpose of sale. The label need not necessarily be attached to or printed on the wrapper or container (s. 15(1)). 'Container' is defined as including any basket, pail, tray, package or receptacle of any kind, whether open or closed (s. 53(1)).

For the offence to be committed this label must either falsely describe the food or be likely to mislead as to its nature of substance or quality.

4.3.1.2 'Falsely' A statement may be literally true but nevertheless be false because of what it omits to state. Under analogous provisions share prospectuses have been held to be false on this basis (*R* v *Kylsant* [1932] 1 KB 442, *R* v *Bishirgian* [1936] 1 All ER 586). A statement can be false even though no gain is made from in (*Jones* v *Meatyard* [1939] 1 All ER 140) and even if the effect of the false statement is disadvantageous to the person making it (*Stevens* v *Evans* [1943] 1 All ER 314). As making a false statement is a strict liability offence, lack of knowledge of the falsity of the offence is no defence (*R* v *Cumerson* [1968] 2 QB 534). Similarly there is no defence even if the defendant believed he had correctly described the food. Thus an offence was committed in *Holmes* v *Piper Ltd* [1914] 1 KB 57 when the description 'British Tarragona wine' was applied to a mixture of 85 per cent wine made from dried English raisins and 15 per cent Mistella, a heavy form of Tarragona wine unsuitable for consumption by itself. In *Kat* v *Diment* [1951] 1 KB 34 it was found to be false to apply the description 'non-brewed vinegar' to acetic acid. This case also held that a description could be false notwithstanding that it was the trade practice so to describe the food. This principle was followed in *Kingston-Upon-Thames Royal London Borough* v *F W Woolworth & Co Ltd* [1968] 1 QB 802. However on the facts of the case a pair of cuff links were found not to be falsely described as being of rolled gold, despite the fact that their back and the connecting chain were not rolled gold. The justices had not simply relied on the alleged trade practice of describing articles as being of rolled gold when in fact only the front was of rolled gold. They had also taken the low price of the cuff links into account. The test of falsity therefore is a question of fact for the magistrates to determine according to what they believe the ordinary man would understand by the description. This was the test applied in *Amos* v *Britvic* (1985) 149 JP 13 when orange juice was found not to have been falsely described as 'natural' despite it having been pasteurised twice, packed in condensed form for shipping and processed by the addition of water.

4.3.1.3 'Likely to mislead' The equivalent provision in the Food Act 1984, s. 6 referred to 'labels calculated to mislead'. The Food Safety Act 1990, s. 15(1) is less stringent in two respects. The need to prove the label was calculated to mislead has been removed. Under the new law it is sufficient that it is likely to mislead. Also it will have been noted that the new wording only requires that the label is likely to mislead, thus emphasising that no one need actually be misled. This seems to have been implicit in the former law where 'mislead' was taken to mean 'likely to mislead'. The Food Act 1984 s. 6(4) had explicitly stated that a label or advertisement calculated to mislead as to the nutritional or dietary value of any food was calculated to mislead as to the quality of the food. This is not reproduced in the Food Safety Act 1990 but is considered to be implicit from the wording of the offence. Whether a label is likely to mislead is a question of fact to be determined by the court on the basis of whether an ordinary person might be misled. This question is not to be answered by relying on an expert witness's evidence, for an ordinary person might be misled where an expert would not have been (*Concentrated Foods Ltd* v *Champ* [1944] KB 342). It would not seem to be necessary to show that anyone was prejudiced (*R* v *Mayling* [1963] 2 QB 717).

4.3.2   Advertisements

It is also an offence for someone to publish, or be party to the publication of, an advertisement which falsely describes any food or is likely to mislead as to the nature or substance or quality of any food (s. 15(2)). The Act defines 'advertisement' as including any notice, circular, label, wrapper, invoice or other document, and any public announcement made orally or by any means of producing or transmitting light or sound (s. 53(1)). However this provision does not apply to a label given or supplied by the defendant which is covered by s. 15(1). Publish means to make public and a fresh publication occurs with each delivery of the advertisement (*Lambert and Lambert* v *Roberts Drug Stores Ltd* [1933] 2 WWR 508).

In respect of both the above offences, relating to labels and advertisements, falsely describing food or being likely to mislead as to its nature or substance or quality, the court shall not be precluded from convicting merely because the label or advertisement contains an accurate statement of the composition of the food (s. 15(4)). This is clearly aimed to ensure there is no loophole for the sharpwitted marketing or advertising consultants to exploit.

4.3.3   Presentation

In similar vein s. 15(3) creates an additional offence aimed at catching those, who although ensuring their advertisements and labels are truthful, nevertheless through other means manage to mislead. The section creates the offence of selling, offering or exposing for sale or having in one's possession for the purpose of sale, any food the presentation of which is likely to mislead as to its nature or substance or quality. The presentation of the food includes its shape, appearance and packaging as well as the way it is arranged when exposed for sale and the setting in which the food is displayed with a view to sale. Any form of labelling or advertising are however excluded from the definition of presentation (s. 53(1)).

4.4   Penalties

If convicted on indictment of an offence under either ss. 14 or 15, a fine and/or imprisonment for up to two years can be imposed. On summary conviction the term of imprisonment cannot exceed six months. The maximum fine on summary conviction for an offence under s. 14 is £20,000 and for an offence under s. 15 is the statutory maximum, currently £2,000.

Chapter Five

Regulations

5.1 Introduction

The Food Safety Act 1990 codifies and stengthens the law relating to food. It is also largely an enabling Act. Sections 16–19 provide wide ranging powers for Ministers to make regulations. The use of delegated legislation is traditional in this area of law and numerous regulations have been enacted under this Act's predecessors, in particular the Food and Drugs Act 1956 and the Food Act 1984. These regulations and orders made under them continue in force (s. 59). Schedule 4 lists the regulations and orders which continue to apply and cites the appropriate provision of the new Act under which they shall be treated as being made.

Regulations or orders are to be made by statutory instrument (s. 48(2)). Both regulations and orders (other than commencement orders) are subject to the negative resolution procedure (s. 48(3)). This means that while Parliament does not have to positively vote to pass the instrument, a proposed instrument can be annulled by resolution of either House of Parliament. Before introducing regulations, Ministers are under a duty to consult organisations which appear to them to be representative of the interests affected (s. 48(4)). This duty to consult does not apply to regulations relating to directly applicable Community provisions or which prohibit the import of specified 'novel foods' (s. 48(4)(a)). The duty to consult does however apply to orders under Part 1 of the Act. These are concerned with the distribution of responsibility for enforcing the Act.

5.2 Food safety and consumer protection

The main regulation-making powers in relation to food safety and consumer protection are provided by the Food Safety Act 1990, s. 16(1). These strengthen, clarify and in some cases extend the previous powers. The powers refer to food but others also cover food sources (see 2.1 and 2.3.1). 'Food' refers to food intended for human consumption and 'food source' refers to food sources from which such food is intended to be derived (s. 16(5)).

Ministers may make regulations:—

(a)   Requiring, prohibiting or regulating the presence in food or food sources of any substance or class of substances (s. 16(1)(a)). 'Substance' is defined to include any natural or artificial substance, whether it is in solid or liquid form or in the form of a gas or vapour (s. 53(1)).

(b)   Regulating, generally, the composition of food (s. 16(1)(a)).

(c)   Securing that food is fit for human consumption (s. 16(1)(b)). This includes being fit for use in the preparation of food for human consumption (s. 53(1)).

(d)   Securing that food meets microbiological standards (s. 16(1)(b)). This covers microbiological standards going to the fitness of food or otherwise; for example, special care may be needed to protect the old or young or to specify the shelf life of products.

(e)   Requiring, prohibiting or regulating the use of any process or treatment in the preparation of food (s. 16(1)(c)). The preparation of food covers its manufacture and any form of processing or treatment (s. 53(1)). Process is not defined by the Act but treatment is specifically said to include subjecting food to heat or cold (s. 53(1)). The most controversial aspect of the Act is the possibility that irradiated food could be permitted to be sold for general consumption. Previously it had only been allowed to be used in hospitals when patients needed special bacteria free diets. The word 'irradiation' appears nowhere in the Act. However it can be regulated as a process. The labelling regulations (see below) can ensure that the fact of irradiation is drawn to the consumer's attention, whilst the premises used for irradiating food can be required to obtain a licence (see 5.7).

(f)   Securing the observance of hygienic conditions and practices in connection with the carrying out of commercial operations with respect to food or food sources (s. 16(1)(d)). Several of the regulation-making powers apply only to 'commercial operations'. This term is defined by s. 1(3) (see 2.3.4).

(g)   Imposing requirements, prohibiting or otherwise regulating the labelling, marking, presenting or advertising of food and the descriptions which may be applied to food (s. 16(1)(e)). 'Labelling' and 'marking' are not defined by the Act but s. 53 does define 'presenting' and 'advertising'. Presentation in relation to food includes its shape, appearance and packaging, the way in which it is arranged when exposed for sale and the setting in which it is displayed with a view to sale. It does not however include any form of labelling or advertising (s. 53(1)). 'Advertising' includes the use of 'any notice, circular, label, wrapper, invoice or other document and any public announcement made orally or by means of producing or transmitting light or sound' (s. 53(1)).

(h)   Making such other provisions, with respect to food or food sources, as appears necessary or expedient:

(i)   to secure compliance with food safety requirements, or

(ii)   is in the interests of public health or

(iii) for the purposes of protecting or promoting the interests of consumers (s. 16(1)(f)).

This is clearly drawn very widely and can be described as a 'catch-all' clause, subject to the proviso that the regulations must be for one or other of the three stated purposes. However the subsection specifically states that once that proviso is satisfied the provision can be made for prohibiting or regulating the carrying out of commercial operations with respect to food or food sources.

When using their regulation-making powers under s. 16(1) Ministers should have regard, so far as practicable, to the desirability of restricting the use of substances of no nutritional value as foods or ingredients in foods (s. 16(4)). This is aimed at restricting the use of additives, such as colourings and preservatives.

Section 16(1) is drawn in very general terms. Without prejudice to that generality, authority is afforded to issue regulations under that section in respect of the matters mentioned in sch. 1 (s. 16(3)). Schedule 1 is subdivided under the followng five sub-headings:—

5.2.1 Composition of food
Regulations can prohibit or regulate the sale, or a range of acts preparatory to sale, of substances or classes of substances with a view to their use in the preparation (see 3.4) of food or the possession of such substances for use in the preparation of food.

5.2.2 Fitness etc of food
Food derived from a food source which is, or is liable to be suffering, or have suffered from any disease can be prohibited from being sold for human consumption or from being used in the manufacture of products for human consumption. Similarly the sale or offer, exposure or distribution for sale for human consumption of shellfish from designated beds or other layings can be prohibited or regulated. The treatment or disposal of food unfit for, or not intended for, or prohibited from being used for human consumption can be regulated. In the case of meat, the enforcement authorities can be given the power to require the premises (see 5.2.4) where meat is sterilised, to be both registered and licensed.

5.2.3 Processing and treatment of food
A process or treatment can be prohibited, unless a person, possessing such qualifications as may be prescribed by the regulations, has made a written opinion with respect to its use in the preparation of food. Also the use of processes and treatments can be prohibited unless a licence has been obtained from the enforcement authority.

5.2.4 Food hygiene
Requirements can be imposed concerning the construction, maintenance, cleanliness and use of food premises, including parts of the premises in which equipment and utensils are cleaned or in which refuse is disposed of or stored. 'Premises' are defined to include any place, vehicle, stall, moveable structure and any ship or aircraft designated for such purposes by Ministerial order (s. 1(3)). Naturally enough 'food premises' means any premises used for the

purposes of a food business and 'food business' means any business in the course of which commercial operations with respect to food or food sources are carried out (s. 1(3), see 2.1, 2.3.1 and 2.3.3). With respect to 'food premises', requirements can be imposed as to the provision, maintenance and cleanliness of sanitary and washing facilities and the disposal of refuse. The responsibility for complying with these requirements can be imposed on the occupier of the premises or, if the requirement is of a structural character, on any owner who either lets the premises for a purpose covered by the regulations or permits them so to be used after notification from the enforcement authorities. It is possible to confer on enforcement authorities the power to issue certificates exempting particular premises from these provisions where compliance cannot reasonably be required.

Regulation-making power also extends to the maintenance and cleanliness of equipment or utensils used for the purposes of a food business and the use of approved cleaning agents on milking equipment.

Under an important new provision, those involved or intending to become involved in food businesses can be required to undergo food hygiene training (Sch. 1 para 5). The regulations can apply to those involved as proprietors, employees or otherwise. By s. 23(1) a food authority may provide, within or outside their area, training courses in food hygiene. The authority can also contribute towards the cost of such training provided by another food authority or other person (s. 23(2)).

5.2.5 Inspection etc of food sources

Provision can be made to secure the inspection, by authorised officers of enforcement authorities, of food sources to ascertain whether they fail to comply with regulations or whether any food derived from the food source is likely to fail to comply with regulations or food safety requirements. The officer can be empowered to give a notice to the person in charge of the food source; such a notice can require that, until a time specified in the notice or until the notice is withdrawn, no commercial operations are carried out with respect to the food source and that the food is not to be removed or is only to be removed to a specified place. This officer can also be empowered, if further investigation reveals the presence of a substance prohibited by regulation in a food source, which is a live animal or bird, to require the slaughter of the animal or bird in question.

5.3 'Contact materials'

Section 16(2) gives Ministers powers to regulate 'contact materials'. These are any articles or substances which are intended to come into contact with food (s. 1(3), see 2.3.2). The definitions of article and substance have already been discussed (see 2.2). This provision would clearly apply, for example, to the cellophane in which food is wrapped, or to the straw through which a drink is consumed. The Act provides generally for prohibiting or regulating the carrying out of commercial operations with respect to such materials (s. 16(2)(c)). More specifically, regulations can provide for securing the observance of hygienic conditions and practices in connection with the carrying out of commercial operations with respect to 'contact materials' which are intended to come into contact with food intended for human consumption (s. 16(2)(a)). The labelling marking, advertising and descriptions which can be applied to such materials can also be subject to regulation and certain conduct can be prohibited or certain requirements can be imposed with regard to these matters (s. 16(2)(b)).

5.4   Enforcement of Community provisions

The European Community has issued a great number of laws relating to food. Some of these laws are directly applicable and become law in the UK without further action. Ministers may pass regulations to secure that a directly applicable Community provision relating to food, food sources or contract materials can be administered, executed and enforced under the Food Safety Act 1990 (s. 17(2)(a)). Regulations may also apply provisions of this Act, possibly with modifications, in relation to Community provisions (s. 17(2)(b)). Other Community laws only become effective after implementation into the domestic law of the member states. The member states are under an obligation to amend their laws to incorporate the European provision. Ministers may issue regulations to meet Community obligations with respect to food, food sources or contact materials (s. 17(1)). In particular the regulations may prohibit or regulate the carrying out of 'commercial operations' (see 2.3.4) with respect to these matters (s. 17(1)). As with the general regulation-making powers of s. 16, references to food are to food intended for sale for human consumption and food sources refer to food sources from which such food is intended to be derived (s. 17(3)).

5.5   Novel foods

Regulations can specify classes of novel foods or food sources from which such foods are intended to be derived and genetically modified food sources or food derived therefrom with respect to which the carrying out of commercial operations and their importation can be prohibited (s. 18(1)(a)-(c)). A 'novel food' means any food which has not previously been used for human consumption in Great Britain, or has been so used only to a very limited extent (s. 18(3)). Novel foods can be divided into two categories. One type consists of 'state of the art' products created using advanced science and technology. Examples of which might be new slimming foods or the so-called 'improved foods' now popular in Japan. The other type's novelty lies not in the fact that it is newly created: it could have existed and been used as a food for centuries; rather the novelty arises because it is new to Great Britain. An example might be an exotic fruit, which has not previously been imported commercially into this country. A food source is considered to be genetically modified if any of the genes or other genetic material in the food source has been modified by an artificial technique or is inherited or otherwise derived, through any number of replications, from genetic material which was so modified (s. 18(4)). For these purposes 'artificial technique' does not include a technique involving no more than, or no more than the assistance of, naturally occurring reproduction processes. Selective breeding techniques or *in vitro* fertilisation are expressly excluded from the definition of 'artificial techniques'. An example of a genetically modified food source currently on sale is genetically modified yeast.

There is power to exlude from these prohibitions food or food scources of specified descriptions (s. 18(1)). In relation to food the description includes any description of its origin or of the manner in which it is packed (s. 18(3)). In respect of prohibitions on importation the exempted food or food source must be imported at an authorised place of entry (s. 18(1)). An authorised place of entry is any port, aerodrome or other place authorised by or under the regulations. If the exemption relates to a particular consignment then the authorised place of entry is any place of entry authorised for the importation of that consignment (s. 18(3)).

It is also relevant to note that the Environmental Protection Bill, currently before Parliament, contains provisions governing 'genetically modified organisms'. This will regulate and impose restrictions on the importation, acquisition, keeping or releasing of such organisms. For present purposes it is important to note that putting products consisting of or including genetically modified organisms on the market is treated as being a release of those organisms.

5.6   Milk

Regulations may give a 'special designation' to milk of any description (s. 18(2)(a)). As noted above in relation to food, description includes any description of its origin or the manner in which it is packed (s. 18(3)). Since milk is a type of of food the same meaning of description will apply in relation to this provision. Enforcement authorities can be empowered to issue licences to producers and sellers of milk authorising the use of a special designation (s. 18(2)(b)). Sales of milk for human consumption, otherwise than with the Minister's consent, can be prohibited unless the special designation is used (s. 18(2)(c)).

5.7   Registration and licensing of food premises

New powers are given to require premises used or proposed to be used for the purpose of a food business to be registered by the enforcement authorities. Any premises not properly registered can be prohibited from being used for a food business (s. 19(1)(a)). This can apply to any premises which are defined to include any place, vehicle, stall, moveable structure and any ship or aircraft designated for such purposes by Ministerial order (s. 1(3)). For the requirement to arise the premises must be used for a 'food business' which means any business in the course of which commercial operations with respect to food or food sources are carried out (see 2.3.3). The wide definition of 'premises' and 'commercial operations' would mean that such businesses as restaurants, roadside caravans selling food, ice cream vendors etc. would be required to register.

The particulars to be entered on the register are to be prescribed by regulations (s. 26(2)(b)). It is likely that the procedure will be quite simple, involving a prescribed form which will ask basic questions concerning the address of the premises, the proprietor's name and the number of employees. It is hoped that the register will allow enforcement officers to build up a clear picture of the food and catering industry in their area and help them to set enforcement priorities. There are powers to require the register to be open to public inspection at all reasonable times and to authorise it to be kept on computer (s. 26(2)(c)). No registration charge is likely to be imposed, although there are powers for so doing (s. 45).

Whereas the registration requirement is likely to be applied to all food businesses, by contrast the power to provide for the issuing by enforcement authorities of licences for premises used or proposed to be used for the purposes of a food business is only likely to be used in respect of a limited range of businesses. The use of premises for food businesses without a licence can be prohibited (s. 19(1)(b)). It is likely that premises used to irradiate food will be licensed. Before requiring licensing, Ministers must believe it is necessary or expedient to do so either for the purposes of securing that food complies with food safety requirements, or because it is in the interests of the public health or for the purpose of protecting or promoting the interests of consumers (s. 19(2)). Regulations will prescribe the licence period and any conditions under which it may be issued as well as providing for the subsequent alteration of the conditions and its possible cancellation, suspension or revocation (s. 26(2)(d)).

5.7.1 Death of registered proprietor or licence holder

In the case of the death of a person registered as proprietor of premises or who held a licence in respect of those premises, the Act permits the registration or licence to subsist temporarily for the benefit of his personal representative, widow or other member of his family. This period of grace ends three months after the death or such longer period as the enforcement authority may allow (s. 43).

5.8 Supplementary provisions

Regulations may prohibit or regulate the carrying out of commercial operations with respect to food, food sources or contact materials which fail to comply with the regulations or in relation to which an offence under the regulations has been committed or would have been committed if the act or omission had taken place in Great Britain (s. 26(1)(a)). Section 26(1)(b) also provides that food caught by s. 26(1)(a) can, by regulation, be treated as failing to satisfy the food safety requirement for the purpose of s. 9 (inspection and seizure of suspected food). Those whose activity is governed by these regulations can also be required to keep and produce records and provide returns (s. 26(2)(a)). Other aspects of the supplementary provisions of s. 26 are dealt with at appropriate parts of the text; one important provision does, however, need to be mentioned. Section 26(3)(a) permits the regulations to specify the way in which an offence under the regulations is to be triable. The regulations can also specify the penalties for which a person guilty of such an offence is liable (s. 26(3)(b)). These may not however exceed those which may be imposed in respect of offences under the Act.

Chapter Six
Defences

6.1 Introduction

It is common in consumer protection statutes to find both strict liability offences and a statutory defence of due diligence. The Food Safety Act is no exception in trying to strike the balance between imposing strict liability whilst exonerating those who have done all they could to prevent the commission of an offence. Section 21 provides a general defence to a defendant who has taken all reasonable precautions and exercised all due diligence. An irrebuttable presumption that the defence is satisfied is available, in some circumstances, to a person charged under ss. 8, 14 and 15 (s. 21(2)). There is also a specific defence of publication in the ordinary course of business (s. 22). A by-pass provision permits a person to be charged whose act or default caused another to commit an offence (s. 20).

The defences in the new Act differ from those available under the Food Act 1984 in two important respects. Firstly, the 1984 Act provided for a defence where the defendant proved the contravention was due to the act or default of another person and that he had used all due diligence to secure that the provisions in question were complied with (s. 100). This was subject to the criticism that it only applied where another party could be blamed for the offence. The new Act simply requires proof of reasonable precautions and due diligence and in that respect is wider than the former defence. It is however the repeal of the so-called 'written warranty defence' provided by the 1984 Act, s. 102 which has caused the food industry the most concern. In order to avail himself of the written warranty defence a defendant had to prove four elements:

(a) that he purchased the goods as being an article or substance which could lawfully be sold or otherwise dealt with;

(b) that he had a written warranty to that effect;

(c) that he had no reason to believe at the time of the commission of the alleged offence that it was otherwise and

(d) that the food was at the time of the alleged offence, in the same state as when he purchased it.

However, it was thought that importers of defective goods could too easily hide behind a warranty and that this was unfair to home producers and manufacturers. Nevertheless, to disallow the use of a warrranty specifically for imports could be construed as a technical barrier to trade contrary to the Treaty of Rome, art. 30. Thus it was decided that the written warranty defence should be repealed and be subsumed under the general due diligence test. This has accordingly been enacted in the 1990 Act, but to mitigate the concerns of the food industry and in order to avoid imposing too onerous a burden on retailers and others who buy in food, the legislation specifies certain circumstances where the defence is deemed to have been satisfied (s. 21(3), (4)).

Ironically, the requirements of the written warranty defence had been more rigourously interpreted in the recent case of *London Borough of Camden* v *Fine Fare Ltd,* 2 February 1987 (unreported). This held that for a large concern like Fine Fare to claim they had no reason to believe that the product had not remained in the same state, from the time they purchased it to the time of sale, they must have some system of checking their products. In that case daily freshness checks on perishable food satisfied the requirement. Notwithstanding this decision, replacing the written warranty defence by the due diligence defence will increase the burden on food businesses. Even the higher standard demanded in the *Fine Fare* case was limited to monitoring the continued accuracy of the warranty and would not involve ascertaining its original veracity by, for example, sampling to check for pesticide traces in food products. There were also hints in the judgment that daily freshness checks could only be expected because the defendant was a large supermarket chain. Under a due diligence test there will be very few instances where the defence will be satisfied by a warranty without any sampling or further checks (see 6.2.1.2). Food retailers and others are, however, assisted in some circumstances by an irrebuttable presumption that the defence is satisfied (see 6.2.5). However, it should be noted that the presumption is not available to either an importer of the food or someone involved in its preparation (s. 21(2)). Also an 'own-brander' must show that he undertook reasonable checks on the food or that it was reasonable for him to rely on checks carried out by his supplier (s. 21(3)). Others have simply to show that they could not reasonably be expected to know their acts or omissions would amount to an offence (s. 21(4)).

6.2 'Due diligence defence'

Various guises of the due diligence defence appear in different statutes. Some versions of the defence simply require due diligence and all reasonable precautions to be shown, whereas others have a preliminary requirement that something such as a mistake, accident or other cause beyond the defendant's control, reliance on information supplied by another or the act or default of another be demonstrated to have caused the commission of the offence. The modern tendency is for the 'due diligence' limb to stand by itself without any preliminary requirement and the Food Safety Act follows this trend. It provides that the defendant should prove that he 'took all reasonable precautions and exercised all due diligence to avoid the commission of the offence by himself or someone under his control' (s. 21(1)). However, although there is no need to demonstrate a specific cause, if the defendant can show the offence was committed due to an act or default of another person who was not under his control or to reliance on information supplied by such a person, then provided certain conditions are fulfilled, the defence of due diligence is deemed to be satisfied in relation to offences under ss. 8, 14 or 15.

6.2.1   Reasonable precautions and all due diligence

O'Keefe suggests that taking 'reasonable precautions' involves 'setting up a system to ensure that things will not go wrong: [and] 'due diligence' means 'seeing that the system works properly'. The defence as formulated in the Food Safety Act does not require a preliminary specific cause to be shown: the specific causes are subsumed within the general test. Whether the defence is made out is a question of fact. Lord Lane LCJ in *Garrett* v *Boots Chemists Ltd,* 16 July 1980 (unreported) said that 'what might be reasonable for a large retailer might not be reasonable for the village shop'. Thus higher standards are to be expected from a large enterprise than from a small business.

6.2.1.1   Variable standards

Although each case turns on its own circumstances, some guidance can be gleaned from the case law. The cases discussed involve a wide range of consumer protection offences but are relevant because they involve similarly worded defences. Relevant factors are 'the nature of the establishment, the sort of articles or goods that are sold, and generally the extent to which a reasonable person would think it right to take the precautions which are being canvassed' (per Lord Widgery in *Ashurst* v *Hayes and Benross Trading Co Ltd,* 9 May 1974 (unreported)). Thus only a relatively low standard could be expected from the two young women in that case who were trying to make a bit of money selling tapes from the back of their car. However no account will be taken of the personal attributes of the defendant. Thus there was no defence for the defendant in *Dennard* v *Abbas* [1987] Crim LR 424 who was an itinerant market trader who usually sold clothes and who spoke very little English and listened to little English music, but who on this occasion sold counterfeit music tapes. He was expected to have made inquiries as to the tapes' genuineness.

A defendant is only expected to do what is reasonable (*Sherratt* v *Gerald The American Jewellers Ltd* (1970) 114 Sol Jo 149), although this simply begs the question: what is reasonable? The defendant is, at the very least, expected to do something! The theory that steps need only be taken if the defendant has been put 'on his guard' was rejected in *R* v *Sheikh,* 9 February 1987 (unreported). The defendant had sold pirate tapes and had made no inquiries as to whether the tapes were legitimate. He argued there was not need for him to take any precautions as there was nothing about the tapes to arouse his suspicions. However the Divisional Court found that he must have been put on guard by the appearance of the tapes. Although technically it is possible to argue that a similar defence might succeed if there was nothing suspicious to put the defendant on his guard, nevertheless a court is likely always to want evidence of some precautions having been taken.

6.2.1.2 Sampling In *Garrett* v *Boots,* 16 July 1980 (unreported) it was found to be insufficient for a defendant simply to inform his supplier of the statutory requirements and obtain a positive assurance from them. This may have been because the case concerned a large retailer, but generally some sampling will be expected. In *Taylor* v *Lawrence Fraser* (1977) 121 Sol Jo 157) Lord Widgery said 'there are very few cases [where] . . . reliance on certificates by itself is to be treated as sufficient when there is the possibility of professional sampling'. The defendants also claimed sampling was impracticable since they were importers and dealt with 3,000 different types of goods but had only 50 staff and it was therefore economically unsound for them to sample each type of goods. This was not accepted by the Divisional Court. The argument that sampling is impractical is valid if the only satisfactory method of sampling is total destruction where each item forms a significant percentage of the total batch. Impracticality on the basis of staff costs is more difficult to justify.

A factor often relied upon by defendants is that they were supplied by a reputable supplier, often one with whom they had had several years of dealing. Although, in some cases, this seems to have been taken into account as one of the relevant circumstances it does not seem to have been decisive in any case; certainly it would rarely stand alone as a defence. It is not clear whether a defendant can rely upon a third party's sampling and checking. Presumably if it was done by someone with whom the defendant had a contractual relationship for the supply of goods it would not be sufficiently independent, but in *Hicks* v *Sullam Ltd* 147 JP 493 the defendants argued that their agents, who had proved satisfactory in the past, were as good as independent electrical engineers. The defence was not accepted because there had been no checks made as to the basis on which the agents made their report. It was also relevant that the agents were outside the jurisdiction and in no danger of finding themselves the subject of proceedings. A similar reluctance to accept foreign analysis was evident in *Rotherham Metropolitan Borough Council* v *Raysun* [1988] BTLC 292 where the sampling was also found to be inadequate because only adverse findings were reported. In that case the court dealt summarily with the argument that the defendant's own sampling of 1 packet of crayons out of the 10,800 dozen packets imported was sufficient. In deciding that the sample was inadequate it was relevant that there was no evidence that a consistent standard could be expected from the batch. Of course even if sampling is not demanded, some system of checking that the goods conform to the order can be expected in nearly every case. This was confirmed recently in *Texas Homecare Ltd* v *Stockport Metropolitan Borough Council* [1987] BTLC 331. This involved a prosecution under the Trade Descriptions Act 1968, for the sale of metal gate valves to which a false trade description, a British Standard mark, had been applied. On appeal the store's conviction was upheld as they had no system for ensuring that the goods delivered to them complied with their description.

6.2.2 Mistake, accident or other cause beyond the defendant's control
Although no specific cause has to be shown to satisfy the due diligence defence in s. 21, the case law on the specific causes remains relevant, for almost any claim of due diligence will seek to establish one of these alternative causes.

Also, proof that the offence was due to the act or default of another person, who was not under the defendant's control, or to information supplied by that person, enables the defendant in some circumtances, to benefit from an irrebuttable presumption that the defence has been made out.

The old case law tended to be concerned with establishing that the mistake was that of the defendant, for otherwise, by pleading mistake rather than act or default of another, the defendant would have been able to circumvent the procedural hurdles which a defendant pleading the latter has to negotiate. There have been no reported cases on the nature of a mistake or accident. O'Keefe however states that:

> This is probably because of the great difficulty for the defendant in establishing the second limb of the defence i.e. that the mistake or accident occurred despite all reasonable precautions and exercising all due diligence. The two limbs of the defence are in this respect almost inherently contradictory.

However, this seems to be wrong, for there is no necessary contradiction between there having been a mistake or accident and all reasonable precautions having been taken and due diligence having been exercised. Rather it is only when all reasonable precautions and due diligence have been taken that something should properly be described as a mistake or an accident.

In *Bibby-Cheshire* v *Golden Wonder Ltd* [1972] 3 All ER 738 a cause beyond the defendant's control was found on evidence that mechanical weighing was necessary because of the scale of the defendant's operation and that despite their having the best machine available it was inevitable that their would be an error in 6 bags out of every 1,000. This can, however, discriminate against small firms. For instance, in *Marshall* v *Herbert* [1963] Crim LR 506 it was conceded that the master baker's staff shortage due to illness was a cause beyond his control but he was not found to have exercised due diligence since he did not weigh each loaf individually. Unusual breakdowns and unlikely defects are said to be bona fide accidents beyond control (*Wolfinden* v *Oliver* (1932) 147 LT 80).

6.2.3   Act or default of another person

The leading case of *Tesco Supermarkets Ltd* v *Nattrass* [1972] AC 153 concerned whether Tesco had taken all reasonable precautions and exercised all due diligence. The House of Lords held that the store manager was 'another person' from the company. In earlier cases a distinction had been drawn between the manager acting in a supervisory capacity in which case he was associated with the business whilst his act in a non-supervisory capacity were acts of another person (see *RC Hammett Ltd* v *Crabb*, *RC Hammett Ltd and Beldam* [1931] All ER Rep 70; *RC Hammett Ltd* v *London County Council* (1933) 97 JP 105; *Beckett* v *Kingston Bros (Butchers)* [1970] 1 QB 606). In *Tesco Supermarkets Ltd* v *Nattrass* the House of Lords took a very narrow view of those actions which could be attributed to the company. The company satisfied the defence of due diligence by the establishment of a satisfactory system and were not responsible for the failure of the manager to implement the system properly. It is said that taking all reasonable precautions involves establishing a system and due diligence involves ensuring the system runs properly. An enterprise the size of Tesco must necessarily devolve some of its day to day supervisory control to managers. This would seem to imply that, if to satisfy the defence the defendant must both establish a system and ensure it runs properly, then the manager is performing the second part of the company's duties and therefore the company should be liable for his actions. Lord Reid however took the view that 'the board never delegated any part of their function. They set up a chain of command through regional and district supervisors, but they remained in control'.

The danger with the *Tesco* v *Nattrass* case is that it can provide businesses with an easy way to escape liability by foisting the responsibility onto its employees who are unlikely to be prosecuted. These fears were expressed by Lord Widgery in *Maguire* v *Sittingbourne Co-operative Society* [1976] Crim LR 268 when he noted:

Unless some little care is taken in regard to these matters, we may find the administration of this Act sliding down to the sort of slip shod level at which all a defendant has to do is to say in general terms that the default must have been due to somebody in the shop, 'one of the girls', or some expression like that, and thereby satisfy the onus cast on him.

Delivering the main judgment in that case Watkins J said that although the defendant need not identify the other person whose act or default was responsible for the offence, he must 'have done all that can reasonably be expected of them by way of inquiry and investigations to find out how the act or default has been committed and who committed it'.

6.2.4   Reliance on information supplied
A defendant can also have a defence if he relied on information supplied by another person. It is presumed that for the defence to apply the source must be one a reasonable person would accept and which would stand up to checking. The cases cited in support of this argument (*Barker* v *Hargreaves* (1980) 125 Sol Jo 165 and *Sutton London Borough* v *Percy Sayger* (1971) 135 JP Jo 239) do reach these conclusions but rather through the application of the requirements of taking reasonable precautions and exercising due diligence. This latter requirement would seem to make the test more stringent than the warranty defence. Although similar requirements were suggested in *Camden London Borough Council* v *Fine Fare Ltd* this was because of the need to ensure the continued accuracy of the warranty, not to test the accuracy of the statement itself.

6.2.5   Retailers and others who buy in food
The due diligence defence in the Food Safety Act is wider than its predecessor in the Food Act 1984, which required proof that the act or default of another caused the offence. Nevertheless the repeal of the written warranty defence caused concern lest retailers and others who buy in food, often pre-packaged, would be held liable for the food although they were not in a position to

54   Defences

control or check the quality of the food. The Act therefore specifies circumstances when they will be deemed to have satisfied the due diligence defence.
This applies to charges under s. 8 (selling food not complying with food safety
requirements), s. 14 (selling food not of the nature, substance or quality
demanded) and s. 15 (falsely describing or presenting food).

This concession is only available to defendants who have neither prepared
nor imported the food concerned (s. 21(2)). The standard demanded of a
defendant to benefit from this irrebuttable presumption of due diligence varies
depending upon whether the seller has applied his own name or mark to the
product. If he has not done so he need only prove that:

(a) the offence was due to the act or default of another who was not under
his control or to reliance on information supplied by that person and
(b) he did not know and could not reasonably be expected to know at the
time of the commission of the alleged offence that his conduct would amount
to an offence (s. 21(4))

An 'own-brander', i.e., someone who sold or intended to sell the food under
his own name or mark (s. 21(4)(b)) must satisfy more stringent requirements.
He must show that the following conditions are all satisfied (see s. 21(3)).

(a) That the offence was due to the act or default of another who was not
under his control, or to reliance on information supplied by that person.
(b) That he carried out all reasonable checks on the food, or that it was
reasonable for him to rely on checks carried out by his supplier.
(c) That he did not know and had no reason to suspect that his act or
omission would amount to an offence.

The aim is clearly to make an own brander responsible for goods sold under
his name or mark; thus paragraph (b) imposes an additional requirement to
those imposed on other sellers. Requirement (c) appears to be more stringent
than the equivalent requirement for a seller other than an own-brander, who
must show only that he had no reasonable grounds to know that his act or
omission would amount to an offence. However, in practice the difference
between the two standards may be more apparent than real. In particular, the
reference in s. 21(4) to 'could not reasonably be expected to know' may import
a requirement to carry out tests on goods sold, the stringency of the testing
required depending on the size and resources of the particular defendant and
on the likelihood of an offence being committed and the seriousness of its
consequences. For instance, it could be argued that a supermarket chain could
reasonably be expected to carry out tests even on branded goods; in that case,
the chain could reasonably be expected to know things which such tests could
reveal. This is in line with existing case law on the meaning of 'due diligence'
in other statutes.

6.2.6 *Notification of defence*
A defendant wishing to rely on the defence that the commission of the offence
was due to an act or default of another person who was not under his control

or to reliance on information supplied by another, must supply the prosecutor (at least seven days before the hearing or within one month of an earlier court appearance in connection with the alleged offence), with a written notice either identifying or giving information to assist in identifying the person who committed the offence (s. 21(5)). Failure to comply with this requirement means that the defendant will not be able to rely on that defence without leave of the court.

6.3   By-pass prosecutions

The person whose act or default caused another to commit an offence can be prosecuted under the 'by-pass' provisions of s. 20, regardless of whether proceedings are brought against the other party. However, if the provisions are given a literal interpretation a loophole could be created. This is because if a person was able to raise a due diligence defence, then it could be argued that nobody could be charged under the by-pass provisions since no actual offence would have been committed. This of course would make the by-pass provisions ineffective, and the courts have given this argument short shrift in cases under similar provisions in other legislation (*Coupe* v *Guyett* [1973] 2 All ER 1058). The position would of course be different if the person originally charged, or liable to be charged, had a defence on the merits.

6.4   Advertisements

A specific defence is provided for publishers and advertising agents where the offence consists of advertising food for sale (s. 22). For the purposes of the Act 'advertisement' is defined to 'include any notice, circular, label, wrapper, invoice or other document, and any public announcement made orally or by any means of producing or transmitting light or sound' (s. 53(1)). To come within the scope of the defence the defendant must be a person whose business is to publish or arrange for the publication of advertisements (s. 22(a)). The defendant must also have received the advertisement in the ordinary course of business and have neither known nor had reason to suspect that it would be illegal to publish it (s. 22(b)). This last requirement of proving lack of knowledge of the illegality of the publication of the advertisement is new and appears to narrow the scope of the defence from that previously found in the 1984 Act, s. 1(3).

Chapter Seven
Enforcement

7.1 Introduction

The efficiency of any statutory control of the quality and safety of consumer goods is dependent upon the enforcement machinery that underpins it. This is as true of food-related legislation as of any other safety-orientated statutory mechanism. The Food Safety Act 1990 has recognised the value of enforcement and addressed the methods by which it may be rendered effective. The provisions contained in the Act include measures to increase the flexibility of enforcement and to extend the scope of statutory control throughout the distribution chain. Hence, a hitherto unknown degree of in-factory enforcement is envisaged with the underlying intention of providing a blanket control from the initial producer to the ultimate user.

7.2 Food authorities

The Act stipulates that, in England and Wales, the food authorities are to be the London borough councils, the district councils and the non-metropolitan county councils (s. 5(1)). In the City of London (including the Temples), power is vested in the Common Council, while in the Inner and Middle Temples the appropriate Treasurer is the enforcement authority. In Scotland enforcement is to be undertaken by the islands or district councils.

The net effect of this provision is that in the non-metropolitan areas of England and Wales, which currently have two tier local government i.e. district councils and county councils, these two councils will have concurrent responsibility for enforcement of the Act. This arrangement gives a large degree of flexibility by permitting duly authorised officers from both tiers of local government to be actively involved in the enforcement of all the Act. However, it could equally be a recipe for confusion and a duplication of effort. The dual enforcement difficulty also arises in the Inner and Middle Temples where both the relevant Treasurers and the Common Council have concurrent responsibility.

This duality of enforcement power mirrors the situation under the Food Act 1984 where officers from both tiers of local government were actively involved in statutory control. Under that Act, the non-metropolitan county councils, in their capacity as food and drugs authorities, were responsible for enforcing certain specified provisions with the district councils being responsible for the remainder. Hence, enforcement involved both Trading Standards Officers, county council employees, and the Environmental Health Officers based at district council level.

The potential undesirability of having two authorities in the same geographic area possessing concurrent enforcement powers is impliedly recognised by s. 5(4) which permits the Minister, by order, to stipulate that one authority shall act alone in the enforcement of the Act, either generally or in relation to cases of a particular nature. It is likely that the Minister will use this power to divide enforcement duties between Environmental Health Officers and Trading Standards Officers.

Section 6(2) provides that every food authority shall enforce and execute the provisions of the Act within their geographic area to the extent that the duty is not imposed either expressly or impliedly upon any other authority. However, under s. 6(3) the Minister has a reserved power to direct that he shall enforce the said duties in relation to cases of a particular description or to a particular case. This would, for example, permit the Minister to intervene either to provide a central coordinating body in a case that involved a large number of enforcement authorities, or, alternatively, to assume the powers of any food authority that was not fulfilling its enforcement role.

Given the multiplicity of enforcement authorities throughout the country, the scope for significant disparity between the enforcement strategies and priorities of differing authorities is obvious. This is, arguably, of lesser importance when authorities are dealing with a small local manufacturer or retailer whose business activities are restricted to one local authority area. The problem increases markedly when the situation involves a larger manufacturer or retailer whose business interests extend nationwide and who may be called upon to deal with several enforcement authorities. This problem is particularly acute in relation to labelling requirements. In a move to provide a uniform standard of enforcement practice nationwide, which would be of benefit both to the consumer and the food industry, s. 40 permits the Minister to issue codes of practice detailing relevant enforcement mechanisms and directions requiring compliance with the code. All authorities would be under a mandatory duty to have regard to any such code and directions when exercising their enforcement functions.

In practice, enforcement authorities act through their 'authorised officers' who are defined as being any person, whether or not an officer of the authority, who is authorised by them in writing to act in their behalf either generally or specially (s. 5(6)). This provision is noticeably broader than the corresponding section of the Food Act 1984 which restricted 'authorised officers' to officers of the council and, in specified situations, to authorised police constables acting with the permission of the police authority. This new provision will introduce a greater degree of flexibility into enforcement by, for example, permitting officers of one authority to be authorised to act on behalf of another. This may be of particular value if food authorities wish to cooperate in investigating a problem.

Taken to its logical conclusion, this definition of 'authorised officer' would permit a food authority to appoint anyone to their enforcement team but the Minister has powers to stipulate that any such enforcement personnel must have prescribed qualifications (s. 5(6)). This will enable him to ensure the continuance of a highly qualified, professional enforcement service by, for example, requiring personnel to possess qualification as an Environmental Health Officer or Trading Standards Officer or requiring them to gain other specialist qualifications such as are currently needed by people involved in the examination of meat.

7.3   Appointment of a public analyst

A major pro-active method of food safety enforcement involves the analysis of food samples to ensure their compliance with statutory standards and regulations. Any such sampling programme necessarily requires that authorised officers have the capacity to procure samples and, further, that an appropriately qualified analyst is availble to undertake the analysis and provide evidence of his findings. In addition to pro-active sampling, the analyst will also have a role to play in reactive analysis in relation to foodstuffs provided by members of the public dissatisfied with their quality.

Sections 27 and 28 detail the duties placed upon some, but not all, food authorities to make provision for the appointment of public analysts and the power given to all food authorities to provide suitable facilities for microbiological examinations.

Section 27, which makes mandatory the appointment of a public analyst, only applies to the London borough councils, the non-metropolitan county councils and the Common Council. In Scotland, a similar duty is placed on the islands and district councils. This requirement accords with the previous situation under the Food Act 1984. The qualification demanded of a public analyst is laid down in the Public Analysts Regulations 1957, which have been adopted by virtue of the Food Safety Act, sch. 4. This stipulates that an analyst must either hold a Diploma of Fellowship or Associateship of the Royal Institution of Chemistry of Great Britain and Ireland, or alternatively have been in post on the 1st January 1970.

There is no requirement that the public analyst must be an officer of the food authority, and thus it is perfectly acceptable for an authority to appoint an independent analyst for this purpose. The only practical restriction placed upon their choice is that the appointee must not be involved either directly or indirectly in any food business carried on within the food authority's area (s. 27(2)). An authority appointing only one public analyst may also appoint a deputy analyst to act during his absence or incapacity, thus ensuring that every food authority should have access to a duly qualified analyst at all times (s. 27(4)). There is nothing to prevent an analyst acting for more than one authority at the same time.

7.4   Analyses and examinations

Section 28 grants all food authorities, at both district council and county council level, the power to provide facilities for examinations undertaken for the purposes of the Act, an examination being defined as a microbiological examination (s. 28(2)). It does not, however, impose a duty so to do. It is noticeable that no reference is made in this section to facilities for analyses, leading to the presumption that the appointment of an analyst must impliedly include the provision of any necessary workplace and equipment, and that there is no need for the statute to deal with the matter separately.

It is important to note that the wording of ss. 29–31 makes clear that the terms 'analysis' and 'examination' are mutually exclusive. 'Analysis' is defined as including 'microbiological assay and any technique for establishing the composition of food' (s. 53(1)). By contrast, the definition of 'examination' makes no reference to the food's composition and thus food may be 'examined' without any intention of identifying its constituent elements. Thus, for example, if the sample is of food allegedly not of the nature, substance or quality demanded in that it is adulterated with a foreign object, such as a metal screw found in a piece of cake, there is no need to analyse the composition of the cake. All that is required is to establish whether the screw was in the cake mixture at the time it was cooked and this can be achieved by considering the extent to which the cake particles adhere to the screw. Thus, an examination would suffice and an analysis would be unnecessary. Conversely, if the intention is to identify the constituent elements of a food product then an analysis is essential and a mere examination would not suffice.

7.5   Procurement of samples

An authorised officer is empowered to procure samples for analysis or examination in two distinct ways, either by purchasing or taking (s. 29). This confirms the decision of the Divisional Court in *Marston* v *Wrington Vale Dairies Ltd* (1963) 61 LGR 202 in which it was held, applying the provisions of the Food and Drugs Act 1955, that a sample of milk which had been purchased, could not be dealt with under a paragraph relating to samples 'taken'. However, depending on the facts of the matter, it may be possible to hold that a sample has been 'taken' even though the officer concerned has subsequently paid the trader the value of the sample (*Southwell* v *Ross* [1945] 2 All ER 590).

Under s. 29 an officer may obtain samples of any food or substance capable of being used in the preparation of food. In view of the definition of 'substances' (see 2.2), flavourings, colourants, anti-oxidants, emulsifiers etc could all be sampled under these provisions. When the sample is obtained by purchase, the officer can acquire a sample of any food, or any substance capable of being used in the preparation of food (s. 29 (a)). By contrast, an officer may only take a sample of food in two situations. First, he may take a sample of any food or substance capable of being used in the preparation of food which appears to him to have been intended for sale, or have been sold, for human consumption (s. 29(b)(i)). In deciding whether this prerequisite has been satisfied, the officer must necessarily make a value judgement based on the surrounding facts. However, he will be aided by the rebuttable presumptions found in s. 3 which provide that any food commonly used for human consumption shall, if sold, offered, exposed or kept for sale be presumed to be intended for sale for human consumption. A similar presumption applies to any substance commonly used in the manufacture of food and found on premises used for the preparation, storage or sale of that food. Secondly, the officer has the power to take a sample of any food or substance capable of being used in the preparation of food found by him on or in any premises to which he has a statutory right of entry (s. 29(b)(ii): for powers of entry see 7.8 below).

In addition to these sampling powers, which re-enact the Food Act 1984, s. 78, the Food Safety Act 1990 has provided new general sampling powers which seek to extend both the situations in which an officer can take samples and the range of products that he can take. Thus, an authorised officer may now take a sample from any food source, or a sample of any contact material, found on or in any premises that he has the power to enter (s. 29(c)). The power to take samples from a food source would obviously allow the taking of a milk sample and might also permit an officer to take (for example) a sample of grain direct from the field to analyse for pesticide residues. The obvious advantage of this extension is that it permits sampling and analysis of products at a far earlier stage of the production process. The provision relating to the sampling of contact materials is equally useful in that it permits the sampling of items, such as packaging, that will come into physical contact with a food product. Such sampling could help deter problems such as those experienced in the past, when it was discovered that some packaging materials caused migration of chemicals into the food.

The final power to take samples involves the right to take samples of any product or substance found in premises to which an officer has a statutory power of entry, if he has reason to believe that it may be needed as evidence in relation to any alleged offence contrary to the Act or any regulations made thereunder (s. 29(d)). The important point to notice is that it relates to any article or substance and not merely food. Therefore the officer may seize anything that he believes will have evidential value.

Throughout this section on sampling powers nothing has been said about the role of enforcement staff in relation to samples of food received from members of the public who, having purchased a food product, have found it to be adulterated or not of the quality demanded and expected. On a strict interpretation of the Act, such products are not samples and, hence, the provisions relating to the sampling powers of authorised officers are not relevant. Under s. 30(2) any person has the right to submit a sample of food that they have purchased directly to the public analyst or food examiner without involving an officer of the food authority. In practice, however, the vast majority of such complainants refer their complaints to the Trading Standards Department or Environmental Health Department, whose officers will process the complaint on the individual's behalf, including submitting the item to the analyst if necessary.

7.6   Sampling procedures

Of prime importance in relation to sampling is the actual procedure by which the product or substance may be validly sampled so as to satisfy any statutory prerequisites and constitute proper evidence in any subsequent hearing. Under the Food Act 1984, detailed sampling requirements were to be found in sch. 7. However, practical difficulties have led to the repeal of that schedule and its replacement by a provision in s. 31 enabling the Minister to make regulations specifying the manner in which samples must be taken. This is, in any case, a matter better dealt with by secondary legislation. The section lists eight different aspects of sampling and analysis, any or all of which may be the subject of such regulations and some of which have been the subject of previous case law. While s. 31(2)(a) refers to matters such as the factors to be taken into account when deciding whether, and at what times, samples should be taken, the crucial and central requirement is arguably that any such regulations can include details of the steps to be taken to ensure that any sample procured is a 'fair sample' (s. 31(2)(b)). This usage of the phrase 'fair sample' impliedly adopts much of the previous case law on sampling in which it has been held that, unless a sample accurately and fairly reflects the constituents of the bulk product being sampled, it cannot be used as the basis for prosecution.

There are two situations in which this requirement is of particular importance, the first being where the bulk being sampled is sufficiently large to demand its storage in several containers. In *Crawford* v *Harding* (1907) SC(J) 11 and *Heatlie* v *Reid* 1961 SLT 317, both Scottish cases relating to the sampling of milk, it was held that in such a situation a prosecution could not be brought in respect of the contents of some rather than all of the containers. This problem can be circumvented by taking samples from all of the relevant containers and then averaging the results to give an accurate analysis of the bulk as a whole (*Wildridge* v *Ashton* [1924] 1 KB 92 and *Lamont* v *Rodger* (1911) SC(J) 24).

The problem of fair sampling may also arise when considering the way in which a sample has been divided for purposes of analysis. Under the Food Act 1984, sch. 7 a sample had to be divided into three parts and a failure to do this correctly would constitute unfair sampling. The difficulty seems most likely to arise with products where it may be numerically simple to split up the sample procured without reference to whether each part is truly representative of the bulk. Thus, for example, in *Skeate* v *Moore* [1971] 3 All ER 1306 the Divisional Court held that when sampling six cornish pasties, it was not sufficient merely to divide them into three lots of two pasties each. The fact that the two pasties analysed by the public analyst were deficient in meat content did not justify a prosecution, as the deficiency in one pie was not evidence of an overall deficiency in the bulk of six. Any prosecution would relate to part of the sample rather than all of it and, as such, would not comply with the statute and hence would be ultra vires. It must be noted that the 1984 Act, s. 84 did provide a statutory exception in that where foodstuffs were contained in unopened containers, and the division of that foodstuff was either impractical or would affect the composition of the foodstuff or impede the analysis of it, then it was acceptable to simply divide the unopened containers into three and treat each portion as a legitimate part of the sample. While the Food Safety Act 1990 does not lay down specific requirements for the division of samples into parts, s. 31(2)(c) does include it as one of the matters about which the Minister may make regulations. It is reasonable to assume that the Minister will make detailed regulations about this aspect of sampling. Section 31(2)(d)–(e) provides the Minister with the power to stipulate to whom parts of the sample and appropriate notices are to be given. Under the Food Act 1984, sch 7, part I one part of the sample was selected and retained by the person from whom the sample had been taken, the second part was submitted to the public analyst for formal analysis, and the third part had to be retained by the food and drugs authority for production in any court hearing. The person from whom the sample was taken was, of course, at liberty to arrange for a private analysis of his portion and use the evidence of such analysis in his defence. The third part could be used in the event of any dispute between the public analyst and any private analyst over the composition or other alleged defect in the product. In such circumstances the court was able to order the analysis of the third part by the Government chemist to provide a definitive analysis of the product upon which the court could then base its decision. In respect of the third part, while ideally it had to be presented to the court in a condition capable of analysis, in practice it did not matter if it had deteriorated to the point where it could not be analysed, the only formal requirement being that it had been properly sealed and duly presented in court (*Winterbottom* v *Allwood* [1915] 2 KB 608, *British Fermentation Products Ltd* v *Teal* [1943] 1 All ER 331). A similar approach to the allocation of parts would seem likely under the Food Safety Act 1990.

As regards the persons to whom notification of the sample must be given, there appears to be a clear deviation from the pre-existing situation. Under the Food Act 1984, s. 80(3) a sampling officer had three days from the time that the sample was procured to send a formal notice to any person whose name and address in the UK was displayed on any appropriate wrapper or container. This applied only if the named person was not entitled to receive a part of the sample and, in practice, covered manufacturers and packers. Such a person was entitled to be told both that the sample had been procured and from whom. By contrast, the Food Safety Act, s. 31(2)(e) limits the regulatory power of the Minister to requiring notification to be given to the person 'in charge' of the food, substance etc sampled. It would be impossible to argue that a manufacturer or packer could be said to be 'in charge' of an item sampled at retail level. Patently, at that stage of the distribution chain, the product has passed out of the control of both manufacturer and packer and, hence, they would have no right to be notified. Thus it appears that the food manufacturer, who may be held liable under the bypass procedure contained in s. 20, may have no right to receive notice that a sample has been taken. Persons in charge of the product and therefore entitled to receive notification would clearly include the person from whom the sample was procured, whether he be a producer, packer, retailer, vendor or, in appropriate circumstances, a consignee. Such people may also be placed under an obligation to furnish specified information presumably to an authorised officer, although, as yet, the relevant detailed regulations have not been promulgated.

7.7 Analysis of samples

Once an officer has procured a sample, whether by purchase or taking, he must decide whether to submit it for analysis or examination. He is under no obligation to do either; it falls within his discretion to decide which procedure, if either, is required. Should he decide that an analysis is called for, he must submit it either to the public analyst for the area in which it was procured or to the public analyst for the area which consists of or includes the area of the authority. This would seem to require authorised officers acting for district councils (who are under no obligation to appoint a public analyst) to submit their samples to the public analyst for the corresponding non-metropolitan county council. Similarly, if an examination seems appropriate, the officer must submit the sample to a food examiner. The Minister has the power to make regulations stipulating in what circumstances a sample is to be submitted to the Government Chemist or to such other food analyst or examiner as he may direct or to a person determined by or under the regulations (s. 31(2)(h)). Under previous legislation there have been officials such as meat examiners who have had responsibility both for the examintion of meat and, if necessary, the recommendation of its condemnation. However, in the present context, the food examiner is envisaged as being an alternative to the public analyst, able to undertake food examinations within the meaning of the Act. Any food examiner may be required to hold such qualifications as are prescribed by the Minister (s. 30(9)). However, there does not appear to be any prima facie objection to the analyst and food examiner being the same person as long as he holds all the relevant qualifications. This would equate with the current situation in which public analysts do undertake examinations of food that fall short of microbiological analysis.

Upon receipt of a sample, the analyst or examiner, as appropriate, must process it as soon as is practicable. Speed is obviously important because of the need to begin any prosecution within the appropriate time limits. Should the public analyst or food examiner be unable to carry out an analysis or examination, the sample must be submitted or sent to such other analyst or examiner as he may determine (s. 30(4)). Further, if the post of public analyst is vacant, a sample must be submitted to the public analyst for some other area (s. 30(3)).

The actual analysis or examination may be undertaken either by the public analyst or food examiner personally or by someone acting under their direction. This would obviously include other analysts, examiners or assistants employed within the laboratory. Section 31(2)(f) gives the Minister power to make regulations specifying the methods that are to be used in the analysis or examination of samples or parts thereof.

The same provision also permits the Minister to dictate the method for classifying the results of analyses and examinations. This is vitally important, for the public analyst's certificate detailing the results of his analysis invariably forms a crucial part of the evidence presented in any prosecution arising from such an analysis. At the moment, the appropriate format is to be found in the schedule to the Public Analysts Regulations 1957, which have been preserved (sch. 4). Therefore, unless the Minister chooses to exercise his powers under

s. 31(2)(f), certificates will continue to be issued in their previous format. A certificate in the appropriate form and signed by the analyst or food examiner must be given to the person who submitted the sample. Thereafter, in any prosecution resulting from the analysis, certain presumptions will arise as to its evidential value. Section 30(8), which reiterates the Food Act 1984, s. 97(1) states that in any proceedings under the Act, the certificate shall be sufficient evidence of the facts contained therein unless the other party requires that the analyst or food examiner be called as a witness. The Divisional Court in *Collins Arden Products Ltd* v *Barking Borough* [1943] KB 419 stipulated that the certificate should be in language that the average person can understand and make clear the offence with which the defendant is being charged. Note that the provision says 'sufficient evidence' not 'conclusive evidence', and thus, even if the defence do not want to put the analyst in the witness box, there is no objection to them introducing evidence that challenges or contradicts the details in the certificate (*Hewitt* v *Taylor* [1986] 1 QB 287). Naturally, in that situation the court is required to balance the evidence given against the facts stated by the analyst. Should the defence fail to introduce contradictory evidence and decline to call the analyst as a witness, the court is then obliged to accept the certificate at face value.

7.8 Powers of entry and obstruction of officers

Consumer and safety-orientated legislation imposing mandatory enforcement functions upon local authorities invariably provides powers of entry for authorised officers engaged in their legitimate duties under the Act. Thus, for example, one finds such powers in both the Trade Descriptions Act 1968 and the Weights and Measures Act 1985 as well as under the Food Act 1984.

The powers of entry and seizure in the Food Safety Act 1990 have made a significant step forward from those contained in the Food Act 1984, in that the new Act includes a power to seize and detain records. This remedies an acknowledged defect in the previous legislation and now brings the enforcement of food safety law more in line with other consumer legislation.

The statutory powers under s. 32(1)(a–b) are vested in authorised officers of the enforcement authority who may be required to produce some duly authenticated document, i.e. a warrant card, at the time of seeking entry. Note that an officer is under no obligation to produce his credentials unless requested to do so, and a failure to do so does not limit either his right to enter or his ability to investigate proceedings as a result of his visit (*Creasey* v *Hoskins,* 1953 (unreported). However, if the officer is requested to show his credentials he must do so or forfeit his powers of entry.

Assuming that these prerequisites are complied with, an officer then has a power to enter all relevant premises within the authority's area for the purpose of ascertaining whether there has been or still is an offence occurring there, contrary to the Act or any regulations or orders made thereunder. Further, he has a power to enter business premises both in and outside the authority's area for the purpose of ascertaining whether any evidence relating to any such offence is on those premises. In addition to these specific powers, there is a general power of entry under s. 32(1)(c) granted to authorised officers of all food authorities to enter any premises for the purposes of performing their statutory functions.

While these powers appear to be very sweeping and undoubtedly facilitate the proper enforcement of the Act, it is important to note the limits upon their scope. Thus, entry may only be demanded during reasonable hours which probably means during normal business hours with due recognition being given to the fact that business hours may vary between differing types of business. Further, if the premises are used only as a dwelling house, entry can only be demanded as of right after giving 24 hours notice. Clearly, notice is not required if the premises are used both as a dwelling house and as business premises. In addition, the prerequisites for exercising the powers of entry are clearly stipulated, namely, the ascertainment of the existence of an offence, or of evidence relating to an offence or of the performance of any authorised function under the Act. Any attempt to use the powers for another purpose would be ultra vires and subject to judicial review. Finally, the powers do not give a right to force an entry, such an eventuality being catered for under s. 32(2) which provides for the issuing of a warrant if entry has been or is likely to be refused.

The powers of entry are a statutory reinforcement of the common law implied licence to enter, which permits anyone with a legitimate purpose to enter premises and remain there for that purpose unless the occupier withdraws permission for them to stay. Thus, in *Brunner* v *Williams* (1975) 73 LGR 266, a case relating to the use of the broadly similar entry powers contained in the Weights and Measures Act 1963 (now repealed), the Divisional Court held that a weights and measures inspector had an implied licence to enter premises to ask the occupier for permission to undertake his statutory enforcement functions therein. If permission is refused or withdrawn, the officer must leave the premises or become a trespasser (*Robson* v *Hallett* [1967] 2 QB 939). Further entry may be effected only with a warrant, granted by a justice of the peace on receipt of written, sworn information that there are reasonable grounds for requiring entry to the premises. Such a warrant is valid for one calendar month, can only be used once and allows the use of reasonable force to gain entry to the premises. Whether entry is by virtue of a warrant or with the consent of the occupier, an authorised officer may be accompanied by any other person he considers necessary, such as an assistant, an authorised officer from another authority or a police officer. On leaving the premises, the officer is under an obligation to ensure that they are as effectively secured as he found them (s. 32(4)).

Having gained entry, an authorised officer may inspect any records relating to a food business and thereafter may seize and detain any records which he has reason to believe may be required as evidence in a case under the provisions of the Act or any orders or regulations made thereunder (s. 32(6)(a)). This is a significant step forward from the previous position where no such power existed. The key word is 'record' and if construed widely may, for instance, include a recipe as being the record of the intended constituent elements of a food product. This interpretation would be particularly valuable in helping officers to establish whether products comply with appropriate labelling and content regulations or were indeed ever intended to comply.

The section gives due cognisance to the increased use of computer records in modern trade by permitting an authorised officer to have access to any computer or associated apparatus or material that has been used in connection with those records. The officer may inspect and check the operation of the equipment requiring any person in charge of it to give him such assistance as he may reasonably require (s. 32(5)). Note that the onus is placed on 'any person' having charge of the computer and not merely upon people suspected of an offence. Therefore any operative is under an obligation to assist or run the risk of prosecution for obstruction. If the officer wishes to seize and detain computer records he may require that they be produced in a form in which he can remove them (s. 32(6)(b)).

As with similar powers under other legislation, s. 32 does not give a power of search but only one of seizure, and renders guilty of an offence any officer who discloses, other than for the performance of his duties, any trade secrets gained by him while on the premises (s. 32(7)).

The intentional obstruction of an enforcement officer is obviously a potentially serious matter and is an offence contrary to s. 33 of the Act. It is important to note that the wording of the obstruction offence has been altered from that previously contained in the Food Act 1984 s. 91. That Act required a 'wilful' obstruction whereas the new provision merely demands an 'intentional' obstruction. This reduces the degree of mens rea needed and thus increases the scope of the offence. In *Rice* v *Connolly* [1966] 2 QB 414, 'wilful' was defined as being conduct that was not merely intentional but without lawful cause, thereby imputing a degree of blameworthy intent. By contrast, in the present context, anyone who acts deliberately, as opposed to accidentally, and whose act is unlawful, will be guilty of an intentional obstruction, even if unaware of the legal implications of their conduct. Obstruction, though never clearly defined, is usually assumed to mean making it more difficult for an officer to carry out his legitimate enforcement functions. This would include refusing him access to premises, physical restraint and failing to fulfil some legal duty.

An offence is also committed if a person, without reasonable cause, fails to provide an officer with any assistance or information that he may reasonably require of them in pursuit of his duties (s. 33(1)(b)). Thus, for example, failing to produce records, or failing to retrieve computer records in a usable form or failing to answer appropriate questions as to the origin or composition of a product would all fall within the ambit of this provision (*Barge* v *British Gas Corporation* (1982) 81 LGR 53). Section 33(2) provides that anyone who knowingly or recklessly provides information which is false or misleading in a material particular will be guilty of an offence. This is an extension to the liability which existed under the Food Act 1984, under which the false information had to have been provided knowingly. This new provision increases the burden on the person giving the information to give due regard to its veracity, for a statement has been held to be made recklessly if the person making it has been careless as to whether it be true or false (*Tesco Supermarkets Ltd* v *Nattrass* [1973] 1 All ER 762).

Naturally, when providing any information or other assistance to an authorised officer, there is no obligation on anyone to answer any question or provide any information which might incriminate himself (s. 33(3)).

7.9 Personal liability of officers

Many of the powers given to authorised officers under the Food Safety Act 1990 require the officer to use his discretion in deciding what action is appropriate. Obvious examples would include the seizing of food under s. 9 and the seizure and subsequent detention of records under s. 32. Efficient enforcement would be seriously hampered if an officer were to feel constantly threatened by the risk of personal liability should he unwittingly make a mistake in the exercise of this discretion. Section 44(1) clearly states that an officer of a food authority is not personally liable in respect of any act done by him which is done both in the execution or purported execution of the Act and falls within the scope of his employment, provided that he acted in the honest belief that his duty required or entitled him to do it. This in no way detracts from the vicarious liability of food authorities for the actions of their officers in such a situation (s. 44(2)). An officer remains personally liable in respect of any actions that he took that were outside the scope of his employment. However, where that is the case, an authority may indemnify him, in whole or part, against both any damages that have been awarded against him or any costs which he has incurred, providing they are satisfied that he honestly believed that the act complained of fell within the course of his employment (s. 44(3)). A public analyst appointed by a food authority receives the protection of this section whether or not his appointment is a whole-time appointment (s. 44(4)).

Chapter Eight
Legal Process

8.1 Introduction

Sections 34–39 deal with the issues relating to criminal process for alleged offences contrary to both the Act and regulations and orders made thereunder. In addition to specifying the grounds and methods of appeal, significant amendments to both limitation periods and penalties have been introduced, which should aid enforcement and encourage compliance.

8.2 Time limits and penalties

Section 34 deals with the time limits for the commencement of any prosecution. With the exception of offences against s. 33(1), the intentional obstruction of an officer or failure to provide assistance reasonably required by him, which attract the standard limitation period of six months specified in the Magistrates Courts Act 1952, all offences contrary to the Food Safety Act 1990 are subject to the time limits specified in s. 34. This stipulates that a prosecution cannot be commenced more than three years from the date of the commission of the offence or one year from its discovery by the prosecutor, whichever is the earlier. The significance of this provision, which follows that contained in the Food Act 1984, s. 95(1) is that it has eschewed the separate shorter time limits that previously applied to prosecutions occurring as a result of sampling. Under the 1984 Act, s. 95(2) where a prosecution resulted from a sample, the relevant time limits were 28 days in the case of milk samples and two months in respect of any other samples. In practice, these periods were simply not long enough to allow for the sample to be procured, analysed, reported upon, investigations undertaken, the decision to prosecute made and legal process begun. Enforcement authorities are bound to welcome the decision to forego these restrictive limitation periods in favour of adopting a uniform approach to all offences relating to the safety of food irrespective of whether it has arisen from a visit to premises, the procurement of a sample or a complaint from a member of the public.

The other significant alteration relates to the penalties that may be imposed under the Act. Under s. 35(1) the offence of intentionally obstructing an officer or failing, without reasonable cause, to provide him with information or assistance, will attract a penalty not exceeding level 5 on the standard scale, currently £2,000. This equates with the fine that could be imposed under the Food Act 1984, s. 91 for the offence of 'wilful obstruction'. Further, as under the previous Act, the obstruction charge is specified as being a summary offence only. However, the penalties relating to the obstruction charges have been strengthened by the introduction of a custodial sentence for an offender. Under s. 35(1) a term of imprisonment not exceeding three months may be imposed instead of or in addition to any fine.

A dramatic rise in the penalties that may be imposed is also seen in relation to the offences that are triable either way (s. 35(2)). When tried on indictment, the penalties remain the imposition of an unlimited fine, or a term of imprisonment not exceeding two years or both. The major alteration occurs in the level of fines that may be imposed upon summary conviction. For offences contrary to ss. 7, 8 and 14, a fine not exceeding £20,000 may now be imposed, which represents a ten fold increase in the financial penalty to which a defendant may be subject. While these increased penalties may reflect the perceived seriousness of food safety offences, it remains to be seen whether the courts will avail themselves of these new higher limits. For all other offences covered by this provision the maximum financial penalty remains at the statutory maximum, currently £2,000 (s. 35(3)). As with the penalties for obstruction, however, s. 35(2) sees the introduction of custodial sentences, a maximum sentence of six months being introduced for all such offences tried summarily. As under s. 35(1), a custodial sentence may be used instead of or in addition to a fine.

The one serious weakness of the new provisions is that, as previously, the penalties for intentional obstruction remain significantly lower than those for some other offences. This may positively encourage a recalcitrant defendant to deliberately obstruct an authorised officer and pay the lower penalty but thereby gain the opportunity to destroy or otherwise dispose of the evidence relating to an offence attracting a heavier penalty. When an obstruction charge carries a £2,000 fine while an offence of selling food not complying with food safety requirements or selling food not of the nature, substance or quality demanded attracts a £20,000 fine, the temptation to obstruct is obvious and must constitute a very real stumbling block to effective enforcement.

The final penalty that may be imposed upon particular defendants is the cancellation of any licence or registration as a knacker's yard or slaughterhouse (s. 35(4)).

8.3   Offences by corporations

Section 36 re-enacts the provision previously contained in the Food Act 1984, s. 93 and found in similar form in many other consumer protection statutes. It provides that where an offence has been committed by a body corporate and it can be shown that the offence was committed with the consent or connivance of various officers of the company, then those officers are personally liable for the offence and can be prosecuted and punished accordingly. This procedure, which recognizes the doctrine of the separate corporate entity, is aimed at that part of the corporate management structure which comprises the directing mind or alter ego of the company. Without it, the directors, company secretary et al would be able to deny all liability for criminal offences committed by the company at their instigation. In interpreting the section, it is clearly established that, in this context, 'manager' means a person involved in the central management of the company and not merely a lower employee such as a branch manager who plays no part in making the central decisions and has no responsibility for them (*Tesco Supermarkets Ltd* v *Nattrass* [1972] AC 153). Under s. 36(1)(b) a person who, although not a director, manager, secretary or similar officer, purported to act in such capacity, may also be held liable in the same way.

The remaining issue is that the offence must have involved the consent or connivance of the defendant. It is suggested that consent presupposes knowledge while connivance merely requires suspicion allied to aquiescence and that actual knowledge may not be essential (*Boulting* v *Boulting* (1864) 3 Sw & Tr 329). Further, it seems likely that negligence would not constitute consent or connivance. Nonetheless, negligence is a relevant concept, as criminal liability may also arise if the company's criminal act is attributable to the neglect of a director or other officer.

8.4   Appeals

The executive power of enforcement authorities to issue improvement notices and control licensing gives them the capacity to affect significantly the trading ability of a food business. It was to be expected, therefore, that the Food Safety Act would provide a mechanism for appeals along similar lines to those found in previous food law. Sections 37–39 specify the process of appeals that may result if an individual is aggrieved by a decision of an enforcement authority and wishes to challenge it, firstly in the magistrates' court and thereafter in the Crown Court.

The appeal system is concerned with three potential grounds of appeal; the issuing of improvement notices, the refusal by an enforcement authority to issue a certificate terminating a prohibition order or emergency prohibition order as provided for under ss. 11(6) and 12(8) respectively, and a decision relating to licensing under Part II of the Act. In respect of the last mentioned, the court does not have jurisdiction if the licensing regulations provide for an appeal to a tribunal.

The appeal is made to the magistrates' court or, in Scotland, to the sheriff by way of summary application, and must be lodged within one month of the date on which the decision complained of was served on the plaintiff, as opposed to the 21 days provided for under the Food Act 1984. In respect of appeals against improvement notices, the period for appeal is either one month or the period mentioned in the improvement notice, whichever ends the earlier (s. 37(5)). In either situation, the decision, when formally served on the plaintiff, must specify both the right to appeal and the period within which the appeal must be lodged (s. 37(6)).

The procedure for appeal, as under the Food Act 1984, is by way of complaint for an order with the Magistrates' Courts Act 1980 applying to the proceedings. It is clear that such an appeal requires a complete rehearing of the case and that it is not sufficient for the court merely to review the grounds of the original decision. Were the court so to restrict itself, an application could be made to the High Court for orders of certiorari to quash its decision and mandamus to force it to rehear the case. It follows that the court may substitute its own decision for that of the enforcement authority.

In respect of an appeal under s. 37(1)(a) against the issuing of an improvement notice, the court may either cancel or affirm the said notice. In choosing to affirm it, the court may then exercise a further discretion as to its terms and either confirm the original notice or substitute such modifications as it thinks fit (s. 39(1)).

Further appeal then lies to the Crown Court, such appeal being restricted to any person 'aggrieved' by the decision of the magistrates' court (s. 38). It seems that this would certainly include a person who is subject to the decision complained of but would not, in all probability, include the enforcement authority. Support for this view may be gained from the permitted grounds of appeal which are limited to dissatisfaction with the decision of the magistrates to dismiss an appeal that they have heard or, alternatively, their decision to impose a prohibition order or emergency prohibition order. Obviously, these grounds of appeal are more appropriate to a plaintiff food business than to an enforcement authority. The final ground of appeal to the Crown Court lies in respect of a decision by the court to cancel the licence or registration of a person trading as a knacker's yard or slaughterhouse, as part of the penalty imposed under s. 35 as the result of a criminal conviction.

8.5 Provisions in regulations

Finally it should be noted that the supplementary powers contained in s. 26 permit regulations to provide:

(a)   For appeals to a magistrates' court, sheriff or other tribunal established by the regulations against any decision of an enforcement authority or one of its officers (s. 26(2)(e)).

(b)   If the regulations establish a tribunal that they can also provide for its procedures (including costs) and for any appeal from its decision (s. 26(2)(f)).

(c)   For the way in which offences under the regulations or orders would be triable (s. 26(3)(a)) and provide that persons guilty of such an offence are liable to penalties not exceeding those for offences under the Act (s. 26(3)(b)).

Food Safety Act 1990

CHAPTER 16

ARRANGEMENT OF SECTIONS

PART I PRELIMINARY

PART II MAIN PROVISIONS

Food safety

Consumer protection

Regulations

Defences etc.

SCHEDULES

Food Safety Act 1990

1990 Chapter 16. An Act to make new provision in place of the Food Act 1984 (except Parts III and V), the Food and Drugs (Scotland) Act 1956 and certain other enactments relating to food; to amend Parts III and V of the said Act of 1984 and Part I of the Food and Environment Protection Act 1985; and for connected purposes.   [29th June 1990]

BE IT ENACTED by the Queen's most Excellent Majesty, by and with the advice and consent of the Lords Spiritual and Temporal, and Commons, in this present Parliament assembled, and by the authority of the same, as follows:—

PART I   PRELIMINARY

Meaning of 'food' and other basic expressions.
1.—(1)   In this Act 'food' includes—
　(a)   drink;
　(b)   articles and substances of no nutritional value which are used for human consumption;
　(c)   chewing gum and other products of a like nature and use; and
　(d)   articles and substances used as ingredients in the preparation of food or anything falling within this subsection.
　(2)   In this Act 'food' does not include—
　(a)   live animals or birds, or live fish which are not used for human consumption while they are alive;
　(b)   fodder or feeding stuffs for animals, birds or fish;
　(c)   controlled drugs within the meaning of the Misuse of Drugs Act 1971; or
　(d)   subject to such exceptions as may be specified in an order made by the Ministers—
　　(i)   medicinal products within the meaning of the Medicines Act 1968 in respect of which product licences within the meaning of that Act are for the time being in force; or

(ii) other articles or substances in respect of which such licences are for the time being in force in pursuance of orders under section 104 or 105 of that Act (application of Act to other articles and substances).

(3) In this Act, unless the context otherwise requires—

'business' includes the undertaking of a canteen, club, school, hospital or institution, whether carried on for profit or not, and any undertaking or activity carried on by a public or local authority;

'commercial operation', in relation to any food or contact material, means any of the following, namely—

(a) selling, possessing for sale and offering, exposing or advertising for sale;

(b) consigning, delivering or serving by way of sale;

(c) preparing for sale or presenting, labelling or wrapping for the purpose of sale;

(d) storing or transporting for the purpose of sale;

(e) importing and exporting;

and, in relation to any food source, means deriving food from it for the purpose of sale or for purposes connected with sale;

'contact material' means any article or substance which is intended to come into contact with food;

'food business' means any business in the course of which commercial operations with respect to food or food sources are carried out;

'food premises' means any premises used for the purposes of a food business;

'food source' means any growing crop or live animal, bird or fish from which food is intended to be derived (whether by harvesting, slaughtering, milking, collecting eggs or otherwise);

'premises' includes any place, any vehicle, stall or moveable structure and, for such purposes as may be specified in an order made by the Ministers, any ship or aircraft of a description so specified.

(4) The reference in subsection (3) above to preparing for sale shall be construed, in relation to any contact material, as a reference to manufacturing or producing for the purpose of sale.

Extended meaning of 'sale' etc.

2.—(1) For the purposes of this Act—

(a) the supply of food, otherwise than on sale, in the course of a business; and

(b) any other thing which is done with respect to food and is specified in an order made by the Ministers,

shall be deemed to be a sale of the food, and references to purchasers and purchasing shall be construed accordingly.

(2) This Act shall apply—

(a) in relation to any food which is offered as a prize or reward or given away in connection with any entertainment to which the public are admitted, whether on payment of money or not, as if the food were, or had been, exposed for sale by each person concerned in the organisation of the entertainment;

(b)   in relation to any food which, for the purpose of advertisement or in furtherance of any trade or business, is offered as a prize or reward or given away, as if the food were, or had been, exposed for sale by the person offering or giving away the food; and

(c)   in relation to any food which is exposed or deposited in any premises for the purpose of being so offered or given away as mentioned in paragraph (a) or (b) above, as if the food were, or had been, exposed for sale by the occupier of the premises;

and in this subsection 'entertainment' includes any social gathering, amusement, exhibition, performance, game, sport or trial of skill.

Presumptions that food intended for human consumption.
3.—(1)   The following provisions shall apply for the purposes of this Act.

(2)   Any food commonly used for human consumption shall, if sold or offered, exposed or kept for sale, be presumed, until the contrary is proved, to have been sold or, as the case may be, to have been or to be intended for sale for human consumption.

(3)   The following, namely—

(a)   any food commonly used for human consumption which is found on premises used for the preparation, storage, or sale of that food; and

(b)   any article or substance commonly used in the manufacture of food for human consumption which is found on premises used for the preparation, storage or sale of that food,

shall be presumed, until the contrary is proved, to be intended for sale, or for manufacturing food for sale, for human consumption.

(4)   Any article or substance capable of being used in the composition or prepration of any food commonly used for human consumption which is found on premises on which that food is prepared shall, until the contrary is proved, be presumed to be intended for such use.

Ministers having functions under Act:
4.—(1)   In this Act—

'the Minister' means, subject to subsection (2) below—

(a)   in relation to England and Wales, the Minister of Agriculture, Fisheries and Food or the Secretary of State;

(b)   in relation to Scotland, the Secretary of State;

'the Ministers' means—

(a)   in relation to England and Wales, the following Ministers acting jointly, namely, the Minister of Agriculture, Fisheries and Food and the Secretaries of State respectively concerned with health in England and food and health in Wales;

(b)   in relation to Scotland, the Secretary of State.

(2)   In this Act, in its application to emergency control orders, 'the Minister' means the Minister of Agriculture, Fisheries and Food or the Secretary of State.

Food authorities and authorised officers.
5.—(1)   Subject to subsections (3) and (4) below, the food authorities in England and Wales are—

(a) as respects each London borough, district or non-metropolitan county, the council of that borough, district or county;

(b) as respects the City of London (including the Temples), the Common Council;

(c) as respects the Inner Temple or the Middle Temple, the appropriate Treasurer.

(2) Subject to subsection (3)(a) below, the food authorities in Scotland are the islands or district councils.

(3) Where any functions under this Act are assigned—

(a) by an order under section 2 or 7 of the Public Health (Control of Disease) Act 1984, to a port health authority or, by an order under section 172 of the Public Health (Scotland) Act 1897, to a port local authority;

(b) by an order under section 6 of the Public Health Act 1936, to a joint board for a united district; or

(c) by an order under paragraph 15(6) of Schedule 8 to the Local Government Act 1985, to a single authority for a metropolitan county,

any reference in this Act to a food authority shall be construed, so far as relating to those functions, as a reference to the authority to whom they are so assigned.

(4) The Ministers may by order provide, either generally or in relation to cases of a particular description, that any functions under this Act which are exercisable concurrently—

(a) as respects a non-metropolitan district, by the council of that district and the council of the non-metropolitan county;

(b) as respects the Inner Temple or the Middle Temple, by the appropriate Treasurer and the Common Council,

shall be exercisable solely by such one of those authorities as may be specified in the order.

(5) In this section—

'the appropriate Treasurer' means the Sub-Treasurer in relation to the Inner Temple and the Under Treasurer in relation to the Middle Temple;

'the Common Council' means the Common Council of the City of London;

'port local authority' includes a joint port local authority.

(6) In this Act 'authorised officer', in relation to a food authority, means any person (whether or not an officer of the authority) who is authorised by them in writing, either generally or specially, to act in matters arising under this Act; but if regulations made by the Ministers so provide, no person shall be so authorised unless he has such qualifications as may be prescribed by the regulations.

Enforcement of Act.
6.—(1) In this Act 'the enforcement authority', in relation to any provisions of this Act or any regulations or orders made under it, means the authority by whom they are to be enforced and executed.

(2) Every food authority shall enforce and execute within their area the provisions of this Act with respect to which the duty is not imposed expressly or by necessary implication on some other authority.

(3)   The Ministers may direct, in relation to cases of a particular description or a particular case, that any duty imposed on food authorities by subsection (2) above shall be discharged by the Ministers or the Minister and not by those authorities.

(4)   Regulations or orders under this Act shall specify which of the following authorities are to enforce and execute them, either generally or in relation to cases of a particular description or a particular area, namely—

(a)   The Ministers, the Minister, food authorities and such other authorities as are mentioned in section 5(3) above; and

(b)   in the case of regulations, the Commissioners of Customs and Excise; and any such regulations or orders may provide for the giving of assistance and information, by any authority concerned in the administration of the regulations or orders, or of any provisions of this Act, to any other authority so concerned, for the purposes of their respective duties under them.

(5)   An enforcement authority in England and Wales may institute proceedings under any provisions of this Act or any regulations or orders made under it and, in the case of the Ministers or the Minister, may take over the conduct of any such proceedings which have been instituted by some other person.

PART II   MAIN PROVISIONS

Food safety

Rendering food injurious to health.
7.—(1)   Any person who renders any food injurious to health by means of any of the following operations, namely—

(a)   adding any article or substance to the food;

(b)   using any article or substance as an ingredient in the preparation of the food;

(c)   abstracting any constituent from the food; and

(d)   subjecting the food to any other process or treatment, with intent that it shall be sold for human consumption, shall be guilty of an offence.

(2)   In determining for the purposes of this section and section 8(2) below whether any food is injurious to health, regard shall be had—

(a)   not only to the probable effect of that food on the health of a person consuming it; but

(b)   also to the probable cumulative effect of food of substantially the same composition on the health of a person consuming it in ordinary quantities.

(3)   In this Part 'injury', in relation to health, includes any impairment, whether permanent or temporary, and 'injurious to health' shall be construed accordingly.

Selling food not complying with food safety requirements.
8.—(1)   Any person who—

(a)   sells for human consumption, or offers, exposes or advertises for sale for such consumption, or has in his possession for the purpose of such sale or of preparation for such sale; or

(b)   deposits with, or consigns to, any other person for the purpose of such sale or of preparation for such sale,
any food which fails to comply with food safety requirements shall be guilty of an offence.

(2)   For the purposes of this Part food fails to comply with food safety requirements if—

(a)   it has been rendered injurious to health by means of any of the operations mentioned in section 7(1) above;

(b)   it is unfit for human consumption; or

(c)   it is so contaminated (whether by extraneous matter or otherwise) that it would not be reasonable to expect it to be used for human consumption in that state;
and references to such requirements or to food complying with such requirements shall be construed accordingly.

(3)   Where any food which fails to comply with food safety requirements is part of a batch, lot or consignment of food of the same class or description, it shall be presumed for the purposes of this section and section 9 below, until the contrary is proved, that all of the food in that batch, lot or consignment fails to comply with those requirements.

(4)   For the purposes of this Part, any part of, or product derived wholly or partly from, an animal—

(a)   which has been slaughtered in a knacker's yard, or of which the carcase has been brought into a knacker's yard; or

(b)   in Scotland, which has been slaughtered otherwise than in a slaughterhouse,
shall be deemed to be unfit for human consumption.

(5)   In subsection (4) above, in its application to Scotland, 'animal' means any description of cattle, sheep, goat, swine, horse, ass or mule; and paragraph (b) of that subsection shall not apply where accident, illness or emergency affecting the animal in question required it to be slaughtered as mentioned in that paragraph.

Inspection and seizure of suspected food.
9.—(1)   An authorised officer of a food authority may at all reasonable times inspect any food intended for human consumption which—

(a)   has been sold or is offered or exposed for sale; or

(b)   is in the possession of, or has been deposited with or consigned to, any person for the purpose of sale or of preparation for sale;
and subsections (3) to (9) below shall apply where, on such an inspection, it appears to the authorised officer that any food fails to comply with food safety requirements.

(2)   The following provisions shall also apply where, otherwise than on such an inspection, it appears to an authorised officer of a food authority that any food is likely to cause food poisoning or any disease communicable to human beings.

(3)   The authorised officer may either—

(a)   give notice to the person in charge of the food that, until the notice is withdrawn, the food or any specified portion of it—

(i)   is not to be used for human consumption; and

(ii)   either is not to be removed or is not to be removed except to some place specified in the notice; or

(b)   seize the food and remove it in order to have it dealt with by a justice of the peace;

and any person who knowingly contravenes the requirements of a notice under paragraph (a) above shall be guilty of an offence.

(4)   Where the authorised officer exercises the powers conferred by subsection (3)(a) above, he shall, as soon as is reasonably practicable and in any event within 21 days, determine whether or not he is satisfied that the food complies with food safety requirements and—

(a)   if he is so satisfied, shall forthwith withdraw the notice;

(b)   if he is not so satisfied, shall seize the food and remove it in order to have it dealt with by a justice of the peace.

(5)   Where an authorised officer exercises the powers conferred by subsection (3)(b) or (4)(b) above, he shall inform the person in charge of the food of his intention to have it dealt with by a justice of the peace and—

(a)   any person who under section 7 or 8 above might by liable to a prosecution in respect of the food shall, if he attends before the justice of the peace by whom the food falls to be dealt with, be entitled to be heard and to call witnesses; and

(b)   that justice of the peace may, but need not, be a member of the court before which any person is charged with an offence under that section in relation to that food.

(6)   If it appears to a justice of the peace, on the basis of such evidence as he considers appropriate in the circumstances, that any food falling to be dealt with by him under this section fails to comply with food safety requirements, he shall condemn the food and order—

(a)   the food to be destroyed or to be so disposed of as to prevent it from being used for human consumption; and

(b)   any expenses reasonably incurred in connection with the destruction or disposal to be defrayed by the owner of the food.

(7)   If a notice under subsection (3)(a) above is withdrawn, or the justice of the peace by whom any food falls to be dealt with under this section refuses to condemn it, the food authority shall compensate the owner of the food for any depreciation in its value resulting from the action taken by the authorised officer.

(8)   Any disputed question as to the right to or the amount of any compensation payable under subsection (7) above shall be determined by arbitration.

(9)   In the application of this section to Scotland—

(a)   any reference to a justice of the peace includes a reference to the sheriff and to a magistrate;

(b)   paragraph (b) of subsection (5) above shall not apply;

(c)   any order made under subsection (6) above shall be sufficient evidence in any proceedings under this Act of the failure of the food in question to comply with food safety requirements; and

(d)   the reference in subsection (8) above to determination by arbitration shall be construed as a reference to determination by a single arbiter appointed, failing agreement between the parties, by the sheriff.

Improvement notices.

10.—(1) If an authorised officer of an enforcement authority has reasonable grounds for believing that the proprietor of a food business is failing to comply with any regulations to which this section applies, he may, by a notice served on that proprietor (in this Act referred to as an 'improvement notice')—

    (a) state the officer's grounds for believing that the proprietor is failing to comply with the regulations;

    (b) specify the matters which constitute the proprietor's failure so to comply;

    (c) specify the measures which, in the officer's opinion, the proprietor must take in order to secure compliance; and

    (d) require the proprietor to take those measures, or measures which are at least equivalent to them, within such period (not being less than 14 days) as may be specified in the notice.

(2) Any person who fails to comply with an improvement notice shall be guilty of an offence.

(3) This section and section 11 below apply to any regulations under this Part which make provision—

    (a) for requiring, prohibiting or regulating the use of any process or treatment in the preparation of food; or

    (b) for securing the observance of hygienic conditions and practices in connection with the carrying out of commercial operations with respect to food or food sources.

Prohibition orders.

11.—(1) If—

    (a) the proprietor of a food business is convicted of an offence under any regulations to which this section applies; and

    (b) the court by or before which he is so convicted is satisfied that the health risk condition is fulfilled with respect to that business,
the court shall by an order impose the appropriate prohibition.

(2) The health risk condition is fulfilled with respect to any food business if any of the following involves risk of injury to health, namely—

    (a) the use for the purposes of the business of any process or treatment;

    (b) the construction of any premises used for the puposes of the business, or the use for those purposes of any equipment; and

    (c) the state or condition of any premises or equipment used for the purposes of the business.

(3) The appropriate prohibition is—

    (a) in a case falling within paragraph (a) of subsection (2) above, a prohibition on the use of the process or treatment for the purposes of the business;

    (b) in a case falling within paragraph (b) of that subsection, a prohibition on the use of the premises or equipment for the purposes of the business or any other food business of the same class or description;

(c)   in a case falling within paragraph (c) of that subsection, a prohibition on the use of the premises or equipment for the purposes of any food business.

(4)   If—

(a)   the proprietor of a food business is convicted of an offence under any regulations to which this section applies by virtue of section 10(3)(b) above; and

(b)   the court by or before which he is so convicted thinks it proper to do so in all the circumstances of the case,

the court may, by an order, impose a prohibition on the proprietor participating in the management of any food business, or any food business of a class or description specified in the order.

(5)   As soon as practicable after the making of an order under subsection (1) or (4) above (in this Act referred to as a 'prohibition order'), the enforcement authority shall—

(a)   serve a copy of the order on the proprietor of the business; and

(b)   in the case of an order under subsection (1) above, affix a copy of the order in a conspicuous position on such premises used for the purposes of the business as they consider appropriate;

and any person who knowingly contravenes such an order shall be guilty of an offence.

(6)   A prohibition order shall cease to have effect—

(a)   in the case of an order under subsection (1) above, on the issue by the enforcement authority of a certificate to the effect that they are satisfied that the proprietor has taken sufficient measures to secure that the health risk condition is no longer fulfilled with respect to the business;

(b)   in the case of an order under subsection (4) above, on the giving by the court of a direction to that effect.

(7)   The enforcement authority shall issue a certificate under paragraph (a) of subsection (6) above within three days of their being satisfied as mentioned in that paragraph; and on an application by the proprietor for such a certificate, the authority shall—

(a)   determine, as soon as is reasonably practicable and in any event within 14 days, whether or not they are so satisfied; and

(b)   if they determine that they are not so satisfied, give notice to the proprietor of the reasons for that determination.

(8)   The court shall give a direction under subsection (6)(b) above if, on an application by the proprietor, the court thinks it proper to do so having regard to all the circumstances of the case, including in particular the conduct of the proprietor since the making of the order; but no such application shall be entertained if it is made—

(a)   within six months after the making of the prohibition order; or

(b)   within three months after the making by the propretor of a previous application for such a direction.

(9)   Where a magistrates' court or, in Scotland, the sheriff makes an order under section 12(2) below with respect to any food business, subsection (1) above shall apply as if the proprietor of the business had been convicted by the court or sheriff of an offence under regulations to which this section applies.

(10)   Subsection (4) above shall apply in relation to a manager of a food business as it applies in relation to the proprietor of such a business; and any reference in subsection (5) or (8) above to the proprietor of the business, or to the proprietor, shall be construed accordingly.

(11)   In subsection (1) above 'manager', in relation to a food business, means any person who is entrusted by the proprietor with the day to day running of the business, or any part of the business.

Emergency prohibition notices and orders.

12.—(1)   If an authorised officer of an enforcement authority is satisfied that the health risk condition is fulfilled with respect to any food business, he may, by a notice served on the proprietor of the business (in this Act referred to as an 'emergency prohibition notice'), impose the appropriate prohibition.

(2)   If a magistrates' court or, in Scotland, the sheriff is satisfied, on the application of such an officer, that the health risk condition is fulfilled with respect to any food business, the court or sheriff shall, by an order (in this Act referred to as an 'emergency prohibition order'), impose the appropriate prohibition.

(3)   Such an officer shall not apply for an emergency prohibition order unless, at least one day before the date of the application, he has served notice on the proprietor of the business of his intention to apply for the order.

(4)   Subsections (2) and (3) of section 11 above shall apply for the purposes of this section as they apply for the purposes of that section, but as if the reference in subsection (2) to risk of injury to health were a reference to imminent risk of such injury.

(5)   As soon as practicable after the service of an emergency prohibition notice, the enforcement authority shall affix a copy of the notice in a conspicuous position on such premises used for the purposes of the business as they consider appropriate; and any person who knowingly contravenes such a notice shall be guilty of an offence.

(6)   As soon as practicable after the making of an emergency prohibition order, the enforcement authority shall—

(a)   serve a copy of the order on the proprietor of the business; and

(b)   affix a copy of the order in a conspicuous position on such premises used for the purposes of that business as they consider appropriate;

and any person who knowingly contravenes such an order shall be guilty of an offence.

(7)   An emergency prohibition notice shall cease to have effect—

(a)   if no application for an emergency prohibition order is made within the period of three days beginning with the service of the notice, at the end of that period;

(b)   if such an application is so made, on the determination or abandonment of the application.

(8)   An emergency prohibition notice or emergency prohibition order shall cease to have effect on the issue by the enforcement authority of a certificate to the effect that they are satisfied that the proprietor has taken sufficient measures to secure that the health risk condition is no longer fulfilled with respect to the business.

(9)   The enforcement authority shall issue a certificate under subsection (8) above within three days of their being satisfied as mentioned in that subsection; and on an application by the proprietor for such a certificate, the authority shall—

(a)   determine, as soon as is reasonably practicable and in any event within 14 days, whether or not they are so satisfied; and

(b)   if they determine that they are not so satisfied, give notice to the proprietor of the reasons for that determination.

(10)   Where an emergency prohibition notice is served on the proprietor of a business, the enforcement authority shall compensate him in respect of any loss suffered by reason of his complying with the notice unless—

(a)   an application for an emergency prohibition order is made within the period of three days beginning with the service of the notice; and

(b)   the court declares itself satisfied, on the hearing of the application, that the health risk condition was fulfilled with respect to the business at the time when the notice was served;

and any disputed question as to the right to or the amount of any compensation payable under this subsection shall be determined by arbitration or, in Scotland, by a single arbiter appointed, failing agreement between the parties, by the sheriff.

Emergency control orders.

13.—(1)   If it appears to the Minister that the carrying out of commercial operations with respect to food, food sources or contact materials of any class or description involves or may involve imminent risk of injury to health, he may, by an order (in this Act referred to as an 'emergency control order'), prohibit the carrying out of such operations with respect to food, food sources or contact materials of that class or description.

(2)   Any person who knowingly contravenes an emergency control order shall be guilty of an offence.

(3)   The Minister may consent, either unconditionally or subject to any condition that he considers appropriate, to the doing in a particlar case of anything prohibited by an emergency control order.

(4)   It shall be a defence for a person charged with an offence under subsection (2) above to show—

(a)   that consent had been given under subsection (3) above to the contravention of the emergency control order; and

(b)   that any condition subject to which that consent was given was complied with.

(5)   The Minister—

(a)   may give such directions as appear to him to be necessary or expedient for the purpose of preventing the carrying out of commercial operations with respect to any food, food sources or contact materials which he believes, on reasonable grounds, to be food, food sources or contact materials to which an emergency control order applies; and

(b)   may do anything which appears to him to be necessary or expedient for that purpose.

(6) Any person who fails to comply with a direction under this section shall be guilty of an offence.

(7) If the Minister does anything by virtue of this section in consequence of any person failing to comply with an emergency control order or a direction under this section, the Minister may recover from that person any expenses reasonably incurred by him under this section.

Consumer protection

Selling food not of the nature or substance or quality demanded.
14.—(1) Any person who sells to the purchaser's prejudice any food which is not of the nature or substance or quality demanded by the purchaser shall be guilty of an offence.

(2) In subsection (1) above the reference to sale shall be construed as a reference to sale for human consumption; and in proceedings under that subsection it shall not be a defence that the purchaser was not prejudiced because he bought for analysis or examination.

Falsely describing or presenting food.
15.—(1) Any person who gives with any food sold by him, or displays with any food offered or exposed by him for sale or in his possession for the purpose of sale, a label, whether or not attached to or printed on the wrapper or container, which—

(a) falsely describes the food; or

(b) is likely to mislead as to the nature or substance or quality of the food,

shall be guilty of an offence.

(2) Any person who publishes, or is a party to the publication of, an advertisement (not being such a label given or displayed by him as mentioned in subsection (1) above) which—

(a) falsely describes any food; or

(b) is likely to mislead as to the nature or substance or quality of any food,

shall be guilty of an offence.

(3) Any person who sells, or offers or exposes for sale, or has in his possession for the purpose of sale, any food the presentation of which is likely to mislead as to the nature or substance or quality of the food shall be guilty of an offence.

(4) In proceedings for an offence under subsection (1) or (2) above, the fact that a label or advertisement in respect of which the offence is alleged to have been committed contained an accurate statement of the composition of the food shall not preclude the court from finding that the offence was committed.

(5) In this section references to sale shall be construed as references to sale for human consumption.

Regulations

Food safety and consumer protection.
16.—(1) The Ministers may by regulations make—

(a)   provision for requiring, prohibiting or regulating the presence in food or food sources of any specified substance, or any substance of any specified class, and generally for regulating the composition of food;

(b)   provision for securing that food is fit for human consumption and meets such microbiological standards (whether going to the fitness of the food or otherwise) as may be specified by or under the regulations;

(c)   provision for requiring, prohibiting or regulating the use of any process or treatment in the preparation of food;

(d)   provision for securing the observance of hygienic conditions and practices in connection with the carrying out of commercial operations with respect to food or food sources;

(e)   provision for imposing requirements or prohibitions as to, or otherwise regulating, the labelling, marking, presenting or advertising of food, and the descriptions which may be applied to food; and

(f)   such other provision with respect to food or food sources, including in particular provision for prohibiting or regulating the carrying out of commercial operations with respect to food or food sources, as appears to them to be necessary or expedient—

(i)   for the purpose of securing that food complies with food safety requirements or in the interests of the public health; or

(ii)   for the purpose of protecting or promoting the interests of consumers.

(2)   The Ministers may also by regulations make provision—

(a)   for securing the observance of hygienic conditions and practices in connection with the carrying out of commercial operations with respect to contact materials which are intended to come into contact with food intended for human consumption;

(b)   for imposing requirements or prohibitions as to, or otherwise regulating, the labelling, marking or advertising of such materials, and the descriptions which may be applied to them; and

(c)   otherwise for prohibiting or regulating the carrying out of commercial operations with respect to such materials.

(3)   Without prejudice to the generality of subsection (1) above, regulations under that subsection may make any such provision as is mentioned in Schedule 1 to this Act.

(4)   In making regulations under subsection (1) above, the Ministers shall have regard to the desirability of restricting, so far as practicable, the use of substances of no nutritional value as foods or as ingredients of foods.

(5)   In subsection (1) above and Schedule 1 to this Act, unless the context otherwise requires—

(a)   references to food shall be construed as references to food intended for sale for human consumption; and

(b)   references to food sources shall be construed as references to food sources from which such food is intended to be derived.

Enforcement of Community provisions.

17.—(1)   The Ministers may by regulations make such provision with respect to food, food sources or contact materials, including in particular provision for prohibiting or regulating the carrying out of commercial operations with respect to food, food sources or contact materials, as appears to them to be called for by any Community obligation.

(2)   As respects any directly applicable Community provision which relates to food, food sources or contact materials and for which, in their opinion, it is appropriate to provide under this Act, the Ministers may by regulations—

(a)   make such provision as they consider necessary or expedient for the purpose of securing that the Community provision is administered, executed and enforced under this Act; and

(b)   apply such of the provisions of this Act as may be specified in the regulations in relation to the Community provision with such modifications, if any, as may be so specified.

(3)   In subsections (1) and (2) above references to food or food sources shall be construed in accordance with section 16(5) above.

Special provisions for particular foods etc.

18.—(1)   The Ministers may by regulations make provision—

(a)   for prohibiting the carrying out of commercial operations with respect to novel foods, or food sources from which such foods are intended to be derived, of any class specified in the regulations;

(b)   for prohibiting the carrying out of such operations with respect to genetically modified food sources, or foods derived from such food sources, of any class so specified; or

(c)   for prohibiting the importation of any food of a class so specified, and (in each case) for excluding from the prohibition any food or food source which is of a description specified by or under the regulations and, in the case of a prohibition on importation, is imported at an authorised place of entry.

(2)   The Ministers may also by regulations—

(a)   prescribe, in relation to milk of any description, such a designation (in this subsection referred to as a 'special designation') as the Ministers consider appropriate;

(b)   provide for the issue by enforcement authorities of licences to producers and sellers of milk authorising the use of a special designation; and

(c)   prohibit, without the use of a special designation, all sales of milk for human consumption, other than sales made with the Minister's consent.

(3)   In this section—

'authorised place of entry' means any port, aerodrome or other place of entry authorised by or under the regulations and, in relation to food in a particular consignment, includes any place of entry so authorised for the importation of that consignment;

'description', in relation to food, includes any description of its origin or of the manner in which it is packed;

'novel food' means any food which has not previously been used for human consumption in Great Britain, or has been so used only to a very limited extent.

(4)   For the purposes of this section a food source is genetically modified if any of the genes or other genetic material in the food source—

(a)   has been modified by means of an artificial technique; or

(b)   is inherited or otherwise derived, through any number of replications, from genetic material which was so modified;
and in this subsection 'artificial technique' does not include any technique which involves no more than, or no more than the assistance of, naturally occurring processes of reproduction (including selective breeding techniques or *in vitro* fertilisation).

Registration and licensing of food premises.
19.—(1)   The Ministers may by regulations make provision—
   (a)   for the registration by enforcement authorities of premises used or proposed to be used for the purposes of a food business, and for prohibiting the use for those purposes of any premises which are not registered in accordance with the regulations; or
   (b)   subject to subsection (2) below, for the issue by such authorities of licences in respect of the use of premises for the purposes of a food business, and for prohibiting the use for those purposes of any premises except in accordance with a licence issued under the regulations.
   (2)   The Ministers shall exercise the power conferred by subsection (1)(b) above only where it appears to them to be necessary or expedient to do so—
   (a)   for the purpose of securing that food complies with food safety requirements or in the interests of the public health; or
   (b)   for the purpose of protecting or promoting the interests of consumers.

Defences etc.

Offences due to fault of another person.
20.   Where the commission by any person of an offence under any of the preceding provisions of this Part is due to an act or default of some other person, that other person shall be guilty of the offence; and a person may be charged with and convicted of the offence by virtue of this section whether or not proceedings are taken against the first-mentioned person.

Defence of due diligence.
21.—(1)   In any proceedings for an offence under any of the preceding provisions of this Part (in this section referred to as 'the relevant provision'), it shall, subject to subsection (5) below, be a defence for the person charged to prove that he took all reasonable precautions and exercised all due diligence to avoid the commission of the offence by himself or by a person under his control.
   (2)   Without prejudice to the generality of subsection (1) above, a person charged with an offence under section 8, 14 or 15 above who neither—
   (a)   prepared the food in respect of which the offence is alleged to have been committed; nor
   (b)   imported it into Great Britain,
shall be taken to have established the defence provided by that subsection if he satisfies the requirements of subsection (3) or (4) below.
   (3)   A person satisfies the requirements of this subsection if he proves—
   (a)   that the commission of the offence was due to an act or default of another person who was not under his control, or to reliance on information supplied by such a person;

(b)   that he carried out all such checks of the food in question as were reasonable in all the circumstances, or that it was reasonable in all the circumstances for him to rely on checks carried out by the person who supplied the food to him; and

(c)   that he did not know and had no reason to suspect at the time of the commission of the alleged offence that his act or omission would amount to an offence under the relevant provision.

(4)   A person satisfies the requirements of this subsection if he proves—

(a)   that the commission of the offence was due to an act or default of another person who was not under his control, or to reliance on information supplied by such a person;

(b)   that the sale or intended sale of which the alleged offence consisted was not a sale or intended sale under his name or mark; and

(c)   that he did not know, and could not reasonably have been expected to know, at the time of the commission of the alleged offence that his act or omission would amount to an offence under the relevant provision.

(5)   If in any case the defence provided by subsection (1) above involves the allegation that the commission of the offence was due to an act or default of another person, or to reliance on information supplied by another person, the person charged shall not, without leave of the court, be entitled to rely on that defence unless—

(a)   at least seven clear days before the hearing; and

(b)   where he has previously appeared before a court in connection with the alleged offence, within one month of his first such appearance,

he has served on the prosecutor a notice in writing giving such information identifying or assisting in the identification of that other person as was then in his possession.

(6)   In subsection (5) above any reference to appearing before a court shall be construed as including a reference to being brought before a court.

Defence of publication in the course of business.
22.   In proceedings for an offence under any of the preceding provisions of this Part consisting of the advertisement for sale of any food, it shall be a defence for the person charged to prove—

(a)   that he is a person whose business it is to publish or arrange for the publication of advertisements; and

(b)   that he received the advertisement in the ordinary course of business and did not know and had no reason to suspect that its publication would amount to an offence under that provision.

Miscellaneous and supplemental

Provision of food hygiene training.
23.—(1)   A food authority may provide, whether within or outside their area, training courses in food hygiene for persons who are or intend to become involved in food businesses, whether as proprietors or employees or otherwise.

(2)   A food authority may contribute towards the expenses incurred under this section by any other such authority, or towards expenses incurred by any other person in providing, such courses as are mentioned in subsection (1) above.

Provision of facilities for cleansing shellfish.

24.—(1) A food authority may provide, whether within or outside their area, tanks or other apparatus for cleansing shellfish.

(2) A food authority may contribute towards the expenses incurred under this section by any other such authority, or towards expenses incurred by any other person in providing, and making available to the public, tanks or other apparatus for cleansing shellfish.

(3) Nothing in this section authorises the establishment of any tank or other apparatus, or the execution of any other work, on, over or under tidal lands below high-water mark of ordinary spring tides, except in accordance with such plans and sections, and subject to such restrictions and conditions as may before the work is commenced be approved by the Secretary of State.

(4) In this section 'cleansing', in relation to shellfish, includes subjecting them to any germicidal treatment.

Orders for facilitating the exercise of functions.

25.—(1) For the purpose of facilitating the exercise of their functions under this Part, the Ministers may by order require every person who at the date of the order, or at any subsequent time, carries on a business of a specified class or description (in this section referred to as a 'relevant business')—

(a) to afford to persons specified in the order such facilities for the taking of samples of any food, substance or contact material to which subsection (2) below applies; or

(b) to furnish to persons so specified such information concerning any such food, substance or contact material,

as (in each case) is specified in the order and is reasonably required by such persons.

(2) This subsection applies to—

(a) any food of a class specified in the order which is sold or intended to be sold in the course of a relevant business for human consumption;

(b) any substance of a class so specified which is sold in the course of such a business for use in the preparation of food for human consumption, or is used for that purpose in the course of such a business; and

(c) any contact material of a class so specified which is sold in the course of such a business and is intended to come into contact with food intended for human consumption.

(3) No information relating to any individual business which is obtained by means of an order under subsection (1) above shall, without the previous consent in writing of the person carrying on the business, be disclosed except—

(a) in accordance with directions of the Minister, so far as may be necessary for the purposes of this Act or of any corresponding enactment in force in Northern Ireland, or for the purpose of complying with any Community obligation; or

(b) for the purposes of any proceedings for an offence against the order or any report of those proceedings;

and any person who discloses any such information in contravention of this subsection shall be guilty of an offence.

(4) In subsection (3) above the reference to a disclosure being necessary for the purposes of this Act includes a reference to it being necessary—

(a) for the purpose of securing that food complies with food safety requirements or in the interests of the public health; or

(b) for the purpose of protecting or promoting the interests of consumers;

and the reference to a disclosure being necessary for the purposes of any corresponding enactment in force in Northern Ireland shall be construed accordingly.

Regulations and orders: supplementary provisions.

26.—(1) Regulations under this Part may—

(a) make provision for prohibiting or regulating the carrying out of commercial operations with respect to any food, food source or contact material—

(i) which fails to comply with the regulations; or

(ii) in relation to which an offence against the regulations has been committed, or would have been committed if any relevant act or omission had taken place in Great Britain; and

(b) without prejudice to the generality of section 9 above, provide that any food which, in accordance with the regulations, is certified as being such food as is mentioned in paragraph (a) above may be treated for the purposes of that section as failing to comply with food safety requirements.

(2) Regulations under this Part may also—

(a) require persons carrying on any activity to which the regulations apply to keep and produce records and provide returns;

(b) prescribe the particulars to be entered on any register required to be kept in accordance with the regulations;

(c) require any such register to be open to inspection by the public at all reasonable times and, subject to that, authorise it to be kept by means of a computer;

(d) prescribe the periods for which and the conditions subject to which licences may be issued, and provide for the subsequent alteration of conditions and for the cancellation, suspension or revocation of licences;

(e) provide for an appeal to a magistrates' court or, in Scotland, to the sheriff, or to a tribunal constituted in accordance with the regulations, against any decision of an enforcement authority, or of an authorised officer of such an authority; and

(f) provide, as respects any appeal to such a tribunal, for the procedure on the appeal (including costs) and for any appeal against the tribunal's decision.

(3) Regulations under this Part or an order under section 25 above may—

(a) provide that an offence under the regulations or order shall be triable in such way as may be there specified; and

(b) include provisions under which a person guilty of such an offence shall be liable to such penalties (not exceeding those which may be imposed in respect of offences under this Act) as may be specified in the regulations or order.

PART III   ADMINISTRATION AND ENFORCEMENT

Administration

Appointment of public analysts.

27.—(1)   Every authority to whom this section applies, that is to say, every food authority in England and Wales and every regional or islands council in Scotland, shall appoint in accordance with this section one or more persons (in this Act referred to as 'public analysts') to act as analysts for the purposes of this Act within the authority's area.

(2)   No person shall be appointed as a public analyst unless he possesses—

(a)   such qualifications as may be prescribed by regulations made by the Ministers; or

(b)   such other qualifications as the Ministers may approve,

and no person shall act as a public analyst for any area who is engaged directly or indirectly in any food business which is carried on in that area.

(3)   An authority to whom this section applies shall pay to a public analyst such remuneration as may be agreed, which may be expressed to be payable either—

(a)   in addition to any fees received by him under this Part; or

(b)   on condition that any fees so received by him are paid over by him to the authority.

(4)   An authority to whom this section applies who appoint only one public analyst may appoint also a deputy to act during any vacancy in the office of public analyst, or during the absence or incapacity of the holder of the office, and—

(a)   the provisions of this section with respect to the qualifications, appointment, removal and remuneration of a public analyst shall apply also in relation to a deputy public analyst; and

(b)   any reference in the following provisions of this Act to a public analyst shall be construed as including a reference to a deputy public analyst appointed under this subsection.

(5)   In subsection (1) above 'food authority' does not include the council of a non-metropolitan district, the Sub-Treasurer of the Inner Temple or the Under Treasurer of the Middle Temple; and in subsection (2) above the reference to being engaged directly or indirectly in a food business includes a reference to having made such arrangements with a food business as may be prescribed by regulations made by the Ministers.

Provision of facilities for examinations.

28.—(1)   A food authority, or a regional council in Scotland, may provide facilities for examinations for the purposes of this Act.

(2)   In this Act 'examination' means a microbiological examination and 'examine' shall be construed accordingly.

Sampling and analysis etc.

Procurement of samples.

29.   An authorised officer of an enforcement authority may—

(a)   purchase a sample of any food, or any substance capable of being used in the preparation of food;

(b)   take a sample of any food, or any such substance, which—

(i)   appears to him to be intended for sale, or to have been sold, for human consumption; or

(ii)   is found by him on or in any premises which he is authorised to enter by or under section 32 below;

(c)   take a sample from any food source, or a sample of any contact material, which is found by him on or in any such premises;

(d)   take a sample of any article or substance which is found by him on or in any such premises and which he has reason to believe may be required as evidence in proceedings under any of the provisions of this Act or of regulations or orders made under it.

Analysis etc. of samples.

30.—(1)   An authorised officer of an enforcement authority who has procured a sample under section 29 above shall—

(a)   if he considers that the sample should be analysed, submit it to be analysed either—

(i)   by the public analyst for the area in which the sample was procured; or

(ii)   by the public analyst for the area which consists of or includes the area of the authority;

(b)   if he considers that the sample should be examined, submit it to be examined by a food examiner.

(2)   A person, other than such an officer, who has purchased any food, or any substance capable of being used in the preparation of food, may submit a sample of it—

(a)   to be analysed by the public analyst for the area in which the purchase was made; or

(b)   to be examined by a food examiner.

(3)   If, in any case where a sample is proposed to be submitted for analysis under this section, the office of public analyst for the area in question is vacant, the sample shall be submitted to the public analyst for some other area.

(4)   If, in any case where a sample is proposed to be or is submitted for analysis or examination under this section, the food analyst or examiner determines that he is for any reason unable to perform the analysis or examination, the sample shall be submitted or, as the case may be, sent by him to such other food analyst or examiner as he may determine.

(5)   A food analyst or examiner shall analyse or examine as soon as practicable any sample submitted or sent to him under this section, but may, except where—

(a)   he is the public analyst for the area in question; and

(b)   the sample is submitted to him for analysis by an authorised officer of an enforcement authority,

demand in advance the payment of such reasonable fee as he may require.

(6)   A food analyst or examiner who has analysed or examined a sample shall give to the person by whom it was submitted a certificate specifying the

result of the analysis or examination.

(7) Any certificate given by a food analyst or examiner under subsection (6) above shall be signed by him, but the analysis or examination may be made by any person acting under his direction.

(8) In any proceedings under this Act, the production by one of the parties—

(a) of a document purporting to be a certificate given by a food analyst or examiner under subsection (6) above; or

(b) of a document supplied to him by the other party as being a copy of such a certificate,

shall be sufficient evidence of the facts stated in it unless, in a case falling within paragraph (a) above, the other party requires that the food analyst or examiner shall be called as a witness.

(9) In this section—

'food analyst' means a public analyst or any other person who possesses the requisite qualifications to carry out analyses for the purposes of this Act;

'food examiner' means any person who possesses the requisite qualifications to carry out examinations for the purposes of this Act;

'the requisite qualifications' means such qualifications as may be prescribed by regulations made by the Ministers, or such other qualifications as the Ministers may approve;

'sample', in relation to an authorised officer of an enforcement authority, includes any part of a sample retained by him in pursuance of regulations under section 31 below;

and where two or more public analysts are appointed for any area, any reference in this section to the public analyst for that area shall be construed as a reference to either or any of them.

Regulation of sampling and analysis etc.

31.—(1) The Ministers may by regulations make provision for supplementing or modifying the provisions of sections 29 and 30 above.

(2) Without prejudice to the generality of subsection (1) above, regulations under that subsection may make provision with respect to—

(a) the matters to be taken into account in determining whether, and at what times, samples should be procured;

(b) the manner of procuring samples, including the steps to be taken in order to ensure that any samples procured are fair samples;

(c) the method of dealing with samples, including (where appropriate) their division into parts;

(d) the persons to whom parts of samples are to be given and the persons by whom such parts are to be retained;

(e) the notices which are to be given to, and the information which is to be furnished by, the persons in charge of any food, substance, contact material or food source of or from which samples are procured;

(f) the methods which are to be used in analysing or examining samples, or parts of samples, or in classifying the results of analyses or examinations;

(g) the circumstances in which a food analyst or examiner is to be precluded, by reason of a conflict of interest, from analysing or examining a particular sample or part of a sample; and

(h) the circumstances in which samples, or parts of samples, are to be or may be submitted for analysis or examination—

(i) to the Government Chemist, or to such other food analyst or examiner as he may direct; or

(ii) to a person determined by or under the regulations.

(3) In this section 'food analyst' and 'food examiner' have the same meanings as in section 30 above.

Powers of entry and obstruction etc.

Powers of entry.

32.—(1) An authorised officer of an enforcement authority shall, on producing, if so required, some duly authenticated document showing his authority, have a right at all reasonable hours—

(a) to enter any premises within the authority's area for the purpose of ascertaining whether there is or has been on the premises any contravention of the provisions of this Act, or of regulations or orders made under it; and

(b) to enter any business premises, whether within or outside the authority's area, for the purpose of ascertaining whether there is on the premises any evidence of any contravention within that area of any of such provisions; and

(c) in the case of an authorised officer of a food authority, to enter any premises for the purpose of the performance by the authority of their functions under this Act;

but admission to any premises used only as a private dwelling-house shall not be demanded as of right unless 24 hours' notice of the intended entry has been given to the occupier.

(2) If a justice of the peace, on sworn information in writing, is satisfied that there is reasonable ground for entry into any premises for any such purpose as is mentiond in subsection (1) above and either—

(a) that admission to the premises has been refused, or a refusal is apprehended, and that notice of the intention to apply for a warrant has been given to the occupier; or

(b) that an application for admission, or the giving of such a notice, would defeat the object of the entry, or that the case is one of urgency, or that the premises are unoccupied or the occupier temporarily absent,

the justice may by warrant signed by him authorise the authorised officer to enter the premises, if need be by reasonable force.

(3) Every warrant granted under this section shall continue in force for a period of one month.

(4) An authorised officer entering any premises by virtue of this section, or of a warrant issued under it, may take with him such other persons as he considers necessary, and on leaving any unoccupied premises which he has entered by virtue of such a warrant shall leave them as effectively secured against unauthorised entry as he found them.

(5) An authorised officer entering premises by virtue of this section, or of a warrant issued under it, may inspect any records (in whatever form they are

held) relating to a food business and, where any such records are kept by means of a computer—

(a) may have access to, and inspect and check the operation of, any computer and any associated apparatus or material which is or has been in use in connection with the records; and

(b) may require any person having charge of, or otherwise concerned with the operation of, the computer, apparatus or material to afford him such assistance as he may reasonably require.

(6) Any officer exercising any power conferred by subsection (5) above may—

(a) seize and detain any records which he has reason to believe may be required as evidence in proceedings under any of the provisions of this Act or of regulations or orders made under it; and

(b) where the records are kept by means of a computer, may require the records to be produced in a form in which they may be taken away.

(7) If any person who enters any premises by virtue of this section, or of a warrant issued under it, discloses to any person any information obtained by him in the premises with regard to any trade secret, he shall, unless the disclosure was made in the performance of his duty, be guilty of an offence.

(8) Nothing in this section authorises any person, except with the permission of the local authority under the Animal Health Act 1981, to enter any premises—

(a) in which an animal or bird affected with any disease to which that Act applies is kept; and

(b) which is situated in a place declared under that Act to be infected with such a disease.

(9) In the application of this section to Scotland, any reference to a justice of the peace includes a reference to the sheriff and to a magistrate.

Obstruction etc. of officers.
33.—(1) Any person who—

(a) intentionally obstructs any person acting in the execution of this Act; or

(b) without reasonable cause, fails to give to any person acting in the execution of this Act any assistance or information which that person may reasonably require of him for the performance of his functions under this Act, shall be guilty of an offence.

(2) Any person who, in purported compliance with any such requirement as is mentioned in subsection (1)(b) above—

(a) furnishes information which he knows to be false or misleading in a material particular; or

(b) recklessly furnishes information which is false or misleading in a material particular, shall be guilty of an offence.

(3) Nothing in subsection (1)(b) above shall be construed as requiring any person to answer any question or give any information if to do so might incriminate him.

Offences

Time limit for prosecutions.
34.   No prosecution for an offence under this Act which is punishable under section 35(2) below shall be begun after the expiry of—
   (a)   three years from the commission of the offence; or
   (b)   one year from its discovery by the prosecutor,
whichever is the earlier.

Punishment of offences.
35.—(1)   A person guilty of an offence under section 33(1) above shall be liable on summary conviction to a fine not exceeding level 5 on the standard scale or to imprisonment for a term not exceeding three months or to both.
   (2)   A person guilty of any other offence under this Act shall be liable—
   (a)   on conviction on indictment, to a fine or to imprisonment for a term not exceeding two years or to both;
   (b)   on summary conviction, to a fine not exceeding the relevant amount or to imprisonment for a term not exceeding six months or to both.
   (3)   In subsection (2) above 'the relevant amount' means—
   (a)   in the case of an offence under section 7, 8 or 14 above, £20,000;
   (b)   in any other case, the statutory maximum.
   (4)   If a person who is—
   (a)   licensed under section 1 of the Slaughterhouses Act 1974 to keep a slaughterhouse or knacker's yard;
   (b)   registered under section 4 of the Slaughter of Animals (Scotland) Act 1980 in respect of any premises for use as a slaughterhouse; or
   (c)   licensed under section 6 of that Act to use any premises as a knacker's yard,
is convicted of an offence under Part II of this Act, the court may, in addition to any other punishment, cancel his licence or registration.

Offences by bodies corporate.
36.—(1)   Where an offence under this Act which has been committed by a body corporate is proved to have been committed with the consent or connivance of, or to be attributable to any neglet on the part of—
   (a)   any director, manager, secretary or other similar officer of the body corporate; or
   (b)   any person who was purporting to act in any such capacity,
he as well as the body corporate shall be deemed to be guilty of that offence and shall be liable to be proceeded against and punished accordingly.
   (2)   In subsection (1) above 'director', in relation to any body corporate established by or under any enactment for the purpose of carrying on under national ownership any industry or part of an industry or undertaking, being a body corporate whose affairs are managed by its members, means a member of that body corporate.

Appeals

Appeals to magistrates' court or sheriff.
37.—(1)   Any person who is aggrieved by—

(a) a decision of an authorised officer of an enforcement authority to serve an improvement notice;

(b) a decision of an enforcement authority to refuse to issue such a certificate as is mentioned in section 11(6) or 12(8) above; or

(c) subject to subsection (2) below, a decision of such an authority to refuse, cancel, suspend or revoke a licence required by regulations under Part II of this Act,

may appeal to a magistrates' court or, in Scotland, to the sheriff.

(2) Subsection (1)(c) above shall not apply in relation to any decision as respects which regulations under Part II of this Act provide for an appeal to a tribunal constituted in accordance with the regulations.

(3) The procedure on an appeal to a magistrates' court under subsection (1) above, or an appeal to such a court for which provision is made by regulations under Part II of this Act, shall be by way of complaint for an order, and the Magistrates' Courts Act 1980 shall apply to the proceedings.

(4) An appeal to the sheriff under subsection (1) above, or an appeal to the sheriff for which provision is made by regulations under Part II of this Act, shall be by summary application.

(5) The period within which such an appeal as is mentioned in subsection (3) or (4) above may be brought shall be—

(a) one month from the date on which notice of the decision was served on the person desiring to appeal; or

(b) in the case of an appeal under subsection (1)(a) above, that period or the period specified in the improvement notice, whichever ends the earlier;

and, in the case of such an appeal as is mentioned in subsection (3) above, the making of the complaint shall be deemed for the purposes of this subsection to be the bringing of the appeal.

(6) In any case where such an appeal as is mentioned in subsection (3) or (4) above lies, the document notifying the decision to the person concerned shall state—

(a) the right of appeal to a magistrates' court or to the sheriff; and

(b) the period within which such an appeal may be brought.

Appeals to Crown Court.
38. A person who is aggrieved by—

(a) any dismissal by a magistrates' court of such an appeal as is mentioned in section 37(3) above; or

(b) any decision of such a court to make a prohibition order or an emergency prohibition order, or to exercise the power conferred by section 35(4) above,

may appeal to the Crown Court.

Appeals against improvement notices.
39.—(1) On an appeal against an improvement notice, the court may either cancel or affirm the notice and, if it affirms it, may do so either in its original form or with such modifications as the court may in the circumstances think fit.

(2) Where, apart from this subsection, any period specified in an improvement notice would include any day on which an appeal against that notice is

pending, that day shall be excluded from that period.

(3)   An appeal shall be regarded as pending for the purposes of subsection (2) above until it is finally disposed of, is withdrawn or is struck out for want of prosecution.

PART IV   MISCELLANEOUS AND SUPPLEMENTAL

Powers of Ministers

Power to issue codes of practice.
40.—(1)   For the guidance of food authorities, the Ministers or the Minister may issue codes of recommended pratice as regards the execution and enforcement of this Act and of regulations and orders made under it; and any such code shall be laid before Parliament after being issued.

(2)   In the exercise of the functions conferred on them by or under this Act, every food authority—

(a)   shall have regard to any relevant provision of any such code; and

(b)   shall comply with any direction which is given by the Ministers or the Minister and requires them to take any specified steps in order to comply with such a code.

(3)   Any direction under subsection (2)(b) above shall, on the application of the Ministers or the Minister, be enforceable by mandamus or, in Scotland, by an order of the Court of Session under section 45 of the Court of Session Act 1988.

(4)   Before issuing any code under this section, the Ministers or the Minister shall consult with such organisations as appear to them or him to be representative of interests likely to be substantially affected by the code.

(5)   Any consultation undertaken before the commencement of subsection (4) above shall be as effective, for the purposes of that subsection, as if undertaken after that commencement.

Power to require returns.
41.   Every food authority shall send to the Minister such reports and returns, and give him such information, with respect to the exercise of the functions conferred on them by or under this Act as he may require.

Default powers.
42.—(1)   Where the Minister is satisfied that—

(a)   a food authority (in this section referred to as 'the authority in default') have failed to discharge any duty imposed by or under this Act; and

(b)   the authority's failure affects the general interests of consumers of food,

he may by order empower another food authority (in this section referred to as 'the substitute authority'), or one of his officers, to discharge that duty in place of the authority in default.

(2)   For the purpose of determining whether the power conferred by subsection (1) above is exercisable, the Minister may cause a local inquiry to be held; and where he does so, the relevant provisions of the Local Government Act shall apply as if the inquiry were a local inquiry held under that Act.

(3)   Nothing in subsection (1) above affects any other power exercisable by the Minister with respect to defaults of local authorities.

(4)   The substitute authority or the Minister may recover from the authority in default any expenses reasonably incurred by them or him under subsection (1) above; and for the purpose of paying any such amount the authority in default may—

(a)   raise money as if the expenses had been incurred directly by them as a local authority; and

(b)   if and to the extent that they are authorised to do so by the Minister, borrow money in accordance with the statutory provisions relating to borrowing by a local authority.

(5)   In this section 'the relevant provisions of the Local Government Act' means subsection (2) to (5) of section 250 of the Local Government Act 1972 in relation to England and Wales and subsections (3) to (8) of section 210 of the Local Government (Scotland) Act 1973 in relation to Scotland.

Protective provisions

Continuance of registration or licence on death.

43.—(1)   This section shall have effect on the death of any person who—

(a)   is registered in respect of any premises in accordance with regulations made under Part II of this Act; or

(b)   holds a licence issued in accordance with regulations so made.

(2)   The registration or licence shall subsist for the benefit of the deceased's personal representative, or his widow or any other member of his family, until the end of—

(a)   the period of three months beginning with his death; or

(b)   such longer period as the enforcement authority may allow.

Protection of officers acting in good faith.

44.—(1)   An officer of a food authority is not personally liable in respect of any act done by him—

(a)   in the execution or purported execution of this Act; and

(b)   within the scope of his employment,

if he did that act in the honest belief that his duty under this Act required or entitled him to do it.

(2)   Nothing in subsection (1) above shall be construed as relieving any food authority from any liability in respect of the acts of their officers.

(3)   Where an action has been brought against an officer of a food authority in respect of an act done by him—

(a)   in the execution or purported execution of this Act; but

(b)   outside the scope of his employment,

the authority may indemnify him against the whole or a part of any damages which he has been ordered to pay or any costs which he may have incurred if they are satisfied that he honestly believed that the act complained of was within the scope of his employment.

(4)   A public analyst appointed by a food authority shall be treated for the purposes of this section as being an officer of the authority, whether or not his appointment is a whole-time appointment.

Financial provisions

Regulations as to charges.

45.—(1) The Ministers may make regulations requiring or authorising charges to be imposed by enforcement authorities in respect of things done by them which they are required or authorised to do by or under this Act.

(2) Regulations under this section may include such provision as the Ministers see fit as regards charges for which the regulations provide and the recovery of such charges; and nothing in the following provisions shall prejudice this.

(3) Regulations under this section may provide that the amount of a charge (if imposed) is to be at the enforcement authority's discretion or to be at its discretion subject to a maximum or a minimum.

(4) Regulations under this section providing that a charge may not exceed a maximum amount, or be less than a minimum amount, may—

    (a) provide for one amount, or a scale of amounts to cover different prescribed cases; and

    (b) prescribe, as regards any amount, a sum or a method of calculating the amount.

Expenses of authorised officers and county councils.

46.—(1) Any expenses which are incurred under this Act by an authorised officer of a food authority in procuring samples, and causing samples to be analysed or examined, shall be defrayed by that authority.

(2) Any expenses incurred by a county council in the enforcement and execution of any provision of this Act, or of any regulations or orders made under it, shall, if the Secretary of State so directs, be defrayed as expenses for special county purposes charged on such part of the county as may be specified in the direction.

Remuneration of tribunal chairmen.

47 There shall be paid out of money provided by Parliament to the chairman of any tribunal consituted in accordance with regulations under this Act such remuneration (by way of salary or fees) and such allowances as the Ministers may with the approval of the Treasury determine.

Instruments and documents

Regulations and orders.

48.—(1) Any power of the Ministers or the Minister to make regulations or an order under this Act includes power—

    (a) to apply, with modifications and adaptations, any other enactment (including one contained in this Act) which deals with matters similar to those being dealt with by the regulations or order;

    (b) to make different provision in relation to different cases or classes of case (including different provision for different areas or different classes of business); and

    (c) to provide for such exceptions, limitations and conditions, and to make such supplementary, incidental, consequential or transitional provisions, as the Ministers or the Minister considers necessary or expedient.

(2)   Any power of the Ministers or the Minister to make regulations or orders under this Act shall be exercisable by statutory instrument.

(3)   Any statutory instrument containing—

(a)   regulations under this Act; or

(b)   an order under this Act other than an order under section 60(3) below,

shall be subject to annulment in pursuance of a resolution of either House of Parliament.

(4)   Before making—

(a)   any regulations under this Act, other than regulations under section 17(2) or 18(1)(c) above; or

(b)   any order under Part I of this Act,

the Ministers shall consult with such organisations as appear to them to be representative of interests likely to be substantially affected by the regulations or order.

(5)   Any consultation undertaken before the commencement of subsection (4) above shall be as effective, for the purposes of that subsection, as if undertaken after that commencement.

Form and authentication of documents.

49.—(1)   The following shall be in writing, namely—

(a)   all documents authorised or required by or under this Act to be given, made or issued by a food authority; and

(b)   all notices and applications authorised or required by or under this Act to be given or made to, or to any officer of, such an authority.

(2)   The Ministers may by regulations prescribe the form of any document to be used for any of the purposes of this Act and, if forms are so prescribed, those forms or forms to the like effect may be used in all cases to which those forms are applicable.

(3)   Any document which a food authority are authorised or required by or under this Act to give, make or issue may be signed on behalf of the authority—

(a)   by the proper officer of the authority as respects documents relating to matters within his province; or

(b)   by any officer of the authority authorised by them in writing to sign documents of the particular kind or, as the case may be, the particular document.

(4)   Any document purporting to bear the signature of an officer who is expressed—

(a)   to hold an office by virtue of which he is under this section empowered to sign such a document; or

(b)   to be duly authorised by the food authority to sign such a document or the particular document,

shall for the purposes of this Act, and of any regulations and orders made under it, be deemed, until the contrary is proved, to have been duly given, made or issued by authority of the food authority.

(5)   In this section—

'proper officer', in relation to any purpose and to any food authority or

any area, means the officer appointed for that purpose by that authority or, as the case may be, for that area;
'signature' includes a facsimile of a signature by whatever process reproduced.

Service of documents.
50.—(1) Any document which is required or authorised by or under this Act to be given to or served on any person may, in any case for which no other provision is made by this Act, be given or served either—

(a) by delivering it to that person;

(b) in the case of any officer of an enforcement authority, by leaving it, or sending it in a prepaid letter addressed to him, at his office;

(c) in the case of an incorporated company or body, by delivering it to their secretary or clerk at their registered or principal office, or by sending it in a prepaid letter addressed to him at that office; or

(d) in the case of any other person, by leaving it, or sending it in a prepaid letter addressed to him, at his usual or last known residence.

(2) Where a document is to be given to or served on the owner or the occupier of any premises and it is not practicable after reasonable inquiry to ascertain the name and address of the person to or on whom it should be given or served, or the premises are unoccupied, the document may be given or served by addressing it to the person concerned by the description of 'owner' or 'occupier' of the premises (naming them) and—

(a) by delivering it to some person on the premises; or

(b) if there is no person on the premises to whom it can be delivered, by affixing it, or a copy of it, to some conspicuous part of the premises.

Amendments of other Acts

Contamination of food: emergency orders.
51.—(1) Part I of the Food and Environment Protection Act 1985 (contamination of food) shall have effect, and shall be deemed always to have had effect, subject to the amendments specified in subsection (2) below.

(2) The amendments referred to in subsection (1) above are—

(a) in subsection (1) of section 1 (power to make emergency orders), the substitution for paragraph (a) of the following paragraph—

'(a) there exist or may exist circumstances which are likely to create a hazard to human health through human consumption of food;';

(b) in subsection (2) of that section, the omission of the definition of 'escape';

(c) the substitution for subsection (5) of that section of the following subsection—

'(5) An emergency order shall refer to the circumstances or suspected circumstances in consequence of which in the opinion of the designating authority making it food such as is mentioned in subsection (1)(b) above is, or may be, or may become, unsuitable for human consumption; and in this Act "designated circumstances" means the circumstances or suspected circumstances to which an emergency order refers in pursuance of this subsection.';

(d)   in section 2(3) (powers when emergency order has been made), the substitution for the words 'a designated incident' of the words 'designated circumstances';

(e)   in paragraph (a) of subsection (1) of section 4 (powers of officers), the substitution for the words 'an escape of substances' of the words 'such circumstances as are mentioned in section 1(1) above'; and

(f)   in paragraphs (b) and (c) of that subsection, the substitution for the words 'the designated incident' of the words 'the designated circumstances'.

Markets, sugar beet and cold storage.
52.   In the Food Act 1984 (in this Act referred to as 'the 1984 Act')—
    (a)   Part III (markets); and
    (b)   Part V (sugar beet and cold storage),
shall have effect subject to the amendments specified in Schedule 2 to this Act.

Supplemental

General interpretation.
53.—(1)   In this Act, unless the context otherwise requires—
    'the 1984 Act' means the Food Act 1984;
    'the 1956 Act' means the Food and Drugs (Scotland) Act 1956;
    'advertisement' includes any notice, circular, label, wrapper, invoice or other document, and any public announcement made orally or by any means of producing or transmitting light or sound, and 'advertise' shall be construed accordingly;
    'analysis' includes microbiological assay and any technique for establishing the composition of food, and 'analyse' shall be construed accordingly;
    'animal' means any creature other than a bird or fish;
    'article' does not include a live animal or bird, or a live fish which is not used for human consumption while it is alive;
    'container' includes any basket, pail, tray, package or receptacle of any kind, whether open or closed;
    'contravention', in relation to any provision, includes any failure to comply with that provision;
    'cream' means that part of milk rich in fat which has been seprated by skimming or otherwise;
    'equipment' includes any apparatus;
    'exportation' and 'importation' have the same meanings as they have for the purposes of the Customs and Excise Management Act 1979, and 'export' and 'import' shall be construed accordingly;
    'fish' includes crustaceans and molluscs;
    'functions' includes powers and duties;
    'human consumption' includes use in the preparation of food for human consumption;
    'knacker's yard' means any premises used in connection with the business of slaughtering, flaying or cutting up animals the flesh of which is not intended for human consumption;
    'milk' includes cream and skimmed or separated milk;
    'occupier', in relation to any ship or aircraft of a description specified in

an order made under section 1(3) above or any vehicle, stall or place, means the master, commander or other person in charge of the ship, aircraft, vehicle, stall or place;

'officer' includes servant;

'preparation', in relation to food, includes manufacture and any form of processing or treatment, and 'preparation for sale' includes packaging, and 'prepare for sale' shall be construed accordingly;

'presentation', in relation to food, includes the shape, appearance and packaging of the food, the way in which the food is arranged when it is exposed for sale and the setting in which the food is displayed with a view to sale, but does not include any form of labelling or advertising, and 'present' shall be construed accordingly;

'proprietor', in relation to a food business, means the person by whom that business is carried on;

'ship' includes any vessel, boat or craft, and a hovercraft within the meaning of the Hovercraft Act 1968, and 'master' shall be construed accordingly;

'slaughterhouse' means a place for slaughtering animals, the flesh of which is intended for sale for human consumption, and includes any place available in connection with such a place for the confinement of animals while awaiting slaughter there or for keeping, or subjecting to any treatment or process, products of the slaughtering of animals there;

'substance' includes any natural or artificial substance or other matter, whether it is in solid or liquid form or in the form of a gas or vapour;

'treatment', in relation to any food, includes subjecting it to heat or cold.

(2) The following Table shows provisions defining or otherwise explaining expressions used in this Act (other than provisions defining or explaining an expression used only in the same section)—

authorised officer of a food authority	section 5(6)
business	section 1(3)
commercial operation	section 1(3) and (4)
contact material	section 1(3)
emergency control order	section 13(1)
emergency prohibition notice	section 12(1)
emergency prohibition order	section 12(2)
enforcement authority	section 6(1)
examination and examine	section 28(2)
food	section 1(1), (2) and (4)
food authority	section 5
food business	section 1(3)
food premises	section 1(3)
food safety requirements and related expressions	section 8(2)
food source	section 1(3)
improvement notice	section 10(1)
injury to health and injurious to health	section 7(3)
the Minister	section 4(1) and (2)
the Ministers	section 4(1)

premises	section 1(3)
prohibition order	section 11(5)
public analyst	section 27(1)
sale and related expressions	section 2
unfit for human consumption	section 8(4)

(3)   Any reference in this Act to regulations or orders made under it shall be construed as a reference to regulations or orders made under this Act by the Ministers or the Minister.

(4)   For the purposes of this Act, any class or description may be framed by reference to any matters or circumstances whatever, including in particular, in the case of a description of food, the brand name under which it is commonly sold.

(5)   Where, apart from this subsection, any period of less than seven days which is specified in this Act would include any day which is—

(a)   a Saturday, a Sunday, Christmas Day or Good Friday; or

(b)   a day which is a bank holiday under the Banking and Financial Dealings Act 1971 in the part of Great Britain concerned,

that day shall be excluded from that period.

Application to Crown.

54.—(1)   Subject to the provisions of this section, the provisions of this Act and of regulations and orders made under it shall bind the Crown.

(2)   No contravention by the Crown of any provision of this Act or of any regulations or order made under it shall make the Crown criminally liable; but the High Court or, in Scotland, the Court of Session may, on the application of an enforcement authority, declare unlawful any act or omission of the Crown which constitutes such a contravention.

(3)   Notwithstanding anything in subsection (2) above, the provisions of this Act and of regulations and orders made under it shall apply to persons in the public service of the Crown as they apply to other persons.

(4)   If the Secretary of State certifies that it appears to him requisite or expedient in the interests of national security that the powers of entry conferred by section 32 above should not be exercisable in relation to any Crown premises specified in the certificate, those powers shall not be exercisable in relation to those premises; and in this subsection 'Crown premises' means premises held or used by or on behalf of the Crown.

(5)   Nothing in this section shall be taken as in any way affecting Her Majesty in her private capacity; and this subsection shall be construed as if section 38(3) of the Crown Proceedings Act 1947 (interpretation of references in that Act to Her Majesty in her private capacity) were contained in this Act.

Water supply: England and Wales.

55.—(1)   Nothing in Part II of this Act or any regulations or order made under that Part shall apply in relation to the supply of water to any premises, whether by a water undertaker or by means of a private supply (within the meaning of Chapter II of Part II of the Water Act 1989).

(2)   In the following provisions of that Act, namely—

section 52 (duties of water undertakers with respect to water quality);

section 53 (regulations for preserving water quality); and

section 64 (additional powers of entry for the purposes of Chapter II), for the words 'domestic purposes', wherever they occur, there shall be substituted the words 'domestic or food production purposes'.

(3) In subsection (2) of section 56 of that Act (general functions of local authorities in relation to water quality), for the words 'domestic purposes' there shall be substituted the words 'domestic or food production purposes' and for the words 'those purposes' there shall be substituted the words 'domestic purposes'.

(4) In subsection (1) of section 57 of that Act (remedial powers of local authorities in relation to private supplies), for the words 'domestic purposes', in the first place where they occur, there shall be substituted the words 'domestic or food production purposes'.

(5) In subsection (1) of section 66 of that Act (interpretation etc. of Chapter II), after the definition of 'consumer' there shall be inserted the following definition—

"'food production purposes" shall be construed in accordance with subsection (1A) below;'.

(6) After that subsection there shall be inserted the following subsection—

'(1A) In this Chapter references to food production purposes are references to the manufacturing, processing, preserving or marketing purposes with respect to food or drink for which water supplied to food production premises may be used; and in this subsection "food production premises" means premises used for the purposes of a business of preparing food or drink for consumption otherwise than on the premises.'

Water supply: Scotland.

56.—(1) Nothing in Part II of this Act or any regulations or order made under that Part shall apply in relation to the supply of water to any premises, whether by a water authority (within the meaning of section 3 of the Water (Scotland) Act 1980) or by means of a private supply (within the meaning of Part VIA of that Act).

(2) In the following provisions of that Act, namely—

section 76A (duties of water authorities with respect to water quality); and

section 76B (regulations for preserving water quality),

for the words 'domestic purposes', wherever they occur, there shall be substituted the words 'domestic or food production purposes'.

(3) In subsection (2) of section 76F of that Act (general functions of local authorities in relation to water quality), for the words 'domestic purposes' there shall be substituted the words 'domestic or food production purposes' and for the words 'those purposes' there shall be substituted the words 'domestic purposes'.

(4) In subsection (1) of section 76G of that Act (remedial powers of local authorities in relation to private supplies), for the words 'domestic purposes', in the first place where they occur, there shall be substituted the words 'domestic or food production purposes'.

(5) In subsection (1) of section 76L of that Act (interpretation etc. of Part VIA), after the definition of 'analyse' there shall be inserted the following definition—

'"food production purposes" shall be construed in accordance with subsection (1A) below;'.

(6) After that subsection there shall be inserted the following subsection—
'(1A) In this Part references to food production purposes are references to the manufacturing, processing, preserving or marketing purposes with respect to food or drink for which water supplied to food production premises may be used; and in this subsection "food production premises" means premises used for the purposes of a business of preparing food or drink for consumption otherwise than on the premises.'

Scilly Isles and Channel Islands.
57.—(1) This Act shall apply to the Isles of Scilly subject to such exceptions and modifications as the Ministers may by order direct.

(2) Her Majesty may by Order in Council direct that any of the provisions of this Act shall extend to any of the Channel Islands with such exceptions and modifications (if any) as may be specified in the Order.

Territorial waters and the continental shelf.
58.—(1) For the purposes of this Act the territorial waters of the United Kingdom adjacent to any part of Great Britain shall be treated as situated in that part.

(2) An Order in Council under section 23 of the Oil and Gas (Enterprise) Act 1982 (application of civil law) may make provision for treating for the purposes of food safety legislation—
(a) any installation which is in waters to which that section applies; and
(b) any safety zone around any such installation,
as if they were situated in a specified part of the United Kingdom and for modifying such legislation in its application to such installations and safety zones.

(3) Such an Order in Council may also confer on persons of a specified description the right to require, for the purpose of facilitating the exercise of specified powers under food safety legislation—
(a) conveyance to and from any installation, including conveyance of any equipment required by them; and
(b) the provision of reasonable accommodation and means of subsistence while they are on any installation.

(4) In this section—
'food safety legislation' means this Act and any regulations and orders made under it and any corresponding provisions in Northern Ireland;
'safety zone' means an area which is a safety zone by virtue of Part III of the Petroleum Act 1987; and
'installation' means an installation to which subsection (3) of the said section 23 applies;
'specified' means specified in the Order in Council.

Amendments, transitional provisions, savings and repeals.
59.—(1) The enactments mentioned in Schedule 3 to this Act shall have effect subject to the amendments there specified (being minor amendments and amendments consequential on the preceding provisions of this Act).

(2) The Ministers may by order make such modifications of local Acts, and of subordinate legislation (within the meaning of the Interpretation Act 1978), as appear to them to be necessary or expedient in consequence of the provisions of this Act.

(3) The transitional provisions and savings contained in Schedule 4 to this Act shall have effect; but nothing in this subsection shall be taken as prejudicing the operation of sections 16 and 17 of the said Act of 1978 (which relate to the effect of repeals).

(4) The enactments mentioned in Schedule 5 to this Act (which include some that are spent or no longer of practical utility) are hereby repealed to the extent specified in the third column of that Schedule.

Short title, commencement and extent.

60.—(1) This Act may be cited as the Food Safety Act 1990.

(2) The following provisions shall come into force on the day on which this Act is passed, namely—

section 13;

section 51; and

paragraphs 12 to 15 of Schedule 2 and, so far as relating to those paragraphs, section 52.

(3) Subject to subsection (2) above, this Act shall come into force on such day as the Ministers may by order appoint, and different days may be appointed for different provisions or for different purposes.

(4) An order under subsection (3) above may make such transitional adaptations of any of the following, namely—

(a) the provisions of this Act then in force or brought into force by the order; and

(b) the provisions repealed by this Act whose repeal is not then in force or so brought into force,

as appear to the Ministers to be necessary or expedient in consequence of the partial operation of this Act.

(5) This Act, except—

this section;

section 51;

section 58(2) to (4); and

paragraphs 7, 29 and 30 of Schedule 3 and, so far as relating to those paragraphs, section 59(1),

does not extend to Northern Ireland.

SCHEDULES

Section 16(3)   **SCHEDULE 1**
PROVISIONS OF REGULATIONS UNDER SECTION 16(1)

Composition of food

1. Provision for prohibiting or regulating—
(a) the sale, possession for sale, or offer, exposure or advertisement for sale, of any specified substance, or of any substance of any specified class, with a view to its use in the preparation of food; or
(b) the possession of any such substance for use in the preparation of food.

Fitness etc. of food

2.—(1) Provision for prohibiting—
(a) the sale for human consumption; or
(b) the use in the manufacture of products for sale for such consumption,
of food derived from a food source which is suffering or has suffered from, or which is liable to be suffering or to have suffered from, any disease specified in the regulations.

(2) Provision for prohibiting or regulating, or for enabling enforcement authorities to prohibit or regulate—
(a) the sale for human consumption; or
(b) the offer, exposure or distribution for sale for such consumption,
of shellfish taken from beds or other layings for the time being designated by or under the regulations.

3.—(1) Provision for regulating generally the treatment and disposal of any food—
(a) which is unfit for human consumption; or
(b) which, though not unfit for human consumption, is not intended for, or is prohibited from being sold for, such consumption.

(2) Provision for the following, namely—
(a) for the registration by enforcement authorities of premises used or proposed to be used for the purpose of sterilising meat to which subparagraph (1) above applies, and for prohibiting the use for that purpose of any premises which are not registered in accordance with the regulations; or
(b) for the issue by such authorities of licences in respect of the use of premises for the purpose of sterilising such meat, and for prohibiting the use for that purpose of any premises except in accordance with a licence issued under the regulations.

Processing and treatment of food

4. Provision for the following, namely—
(a) for the giving by persons possessing such qualifications as may be prescribed by the regulations of written opinions with respect to the use of any

process or treatment in the preparation of food, and for prohibiting the use for any such purpose of any process or treatment except in accordance with an opinion given under the regulations; or

(b) for the issue by enforcement authorities of licences in respect of the use of any process or treatment in the preparation of food, and for prohibiting the use for any such purpose of any process or treatment except in accordance with a licence issued under the regulations.

Food hygiene

5.—(1) Provision for imposing requirements as to —

(a) the construction, maintenance, cleanliness and use of food premises, including any parts of such premises in which equipment and utensils are cleaned, or in which refuse is disposed of or stored;

(b) the provision, maintenance and cleanliness of sanitary and washing facilities in connection with such premises; and

(c) the disposal of refuse from such premises.

(2) Provision for imposing requirements as to—

(a) the maintenance and cleanliness of equipment or utensils used for the purposes of a food business; and

(b) the use, for the cleaning of equipment used for milking, of cleaning agents approved by or under the regulations.

(3) Provision for requiring persons who are or intend to become involved in food businesses, whether as proprietors or employees or otherwise, to undergo such food hygiene training as may be specified in the regulations.

6.—(1) Provision for imposing responsibility for compliance with any requirements imposed by virtue of paragraph 5(1) above in respect of any premises—

(a) on the occupier of the premises; and

(b) in the case of requirements of a structural character, on any owner of the premises who either—

(i) lets them for use for a purpose to which the regulations apply; or

(ii) permits them to be so used after notice from the authority charged with the enforcement of the regulations.

(2) Provision for conferring in relation to particular premises, subject to such limitations and safeguards as may be specified, exemptions from the operation of specified provisions which—

(a) are contained in the regulations; and

(b) are made by virtue of paragraph 5(1) above,

while there is in force a certificate of the enforcement authority to the effect that compliance with those provisions cannot reasonably be required with respect to the premises or any activities carried on in them.

Inspection etc. of food sources

7.—(1) Provision for securing the inspection of food sources by authorised officers of enforcement authorities for the purpose of ascertaining whether they—

(a) fail to comply with the requirements of the regulations; or

(b) are such that any food derived from them is likely to fail to comply with those requirements.

(2) Provision for enabling such an officer, if it appears to him on such an inspection that any food source falls within sub-paragraph (1)(a) or (b) above, to give notice to the person in charge of the food source that, until a time specified in the notice or until the notice is withdrawn—

(a) no commercial operations are to be carried out with respect to the food source; and

(b) the food source either is not to be removed or is not to be removed except to some place so specified.

(3) Provision for enabling such an officer, if on further investigation it appears to him, in the case of any such food source which is a live animal or bird, that there is present in the animal or bird any substance whose presence is prohibited by the regulations, to cause the animal or bird to be slaughtered.

Section 52.   SCHEDULE 2

AMENDMENT OF PARTS III AND V OF 1984 ACT

Amendments of Part III

1. Part III of the 1984 Act (markets) shall be amended in accordance with paragraphs 2 to 11 below.

2.—(1) In subsection (1) of section 50 (establishment or acquisition of markets), for the words 'The council of a district' there shall be substituted the words 'A local authority' and for the words 'their district', in each place where they occur, there shall be substituted the words 'their area'.

(2) In subsection (2) of that section, for the words 'the district' there shall be substituted the words 'the authority's area'.

(3) For subsection (3) of that section there shall be substituted the following subsection—

'(3) For the purposes of subsection (2), a local authority shall not be regarded as enjoying any rights, powers or privileges within another local authority's area by reason only of the fact that they maintain within their own area a market which has been established under paragraph (a) of subsection (1) or under the corresponding provision of any earlier enactment'.

3. In section 51(2) (power to sell to local authority), the word 'market' shall cease to have effect.

4.—(1) In subsection (1) of section 53 (charges by market authority), the words 'and in respect of the weighing and measuring of articles and vehicles' shall cease to have effect.

(2) For subsection (2) of that section there shall be substituted the following subsection—

'(2) A market authority who provide—

(a) a weighing machine for weighing cattle, sheep or swine; or

(b) a cold air store or refrigerator for the storage and preservation

of meat and other articles of food,
may demand in respect of the weighing of such animals or, as the case
may be, the use of the store or refrigerator such charges as they may from
time to time determine.'

(3) In subsection (3)(b) of that section, the words 'in respect of the
weighing of vehicles, or, as the case may be,' shall cease to have effect.

5. For subsection (2) of section 54 (time for payment of charges) there shall
be substituted the following subsection—

'(2) Charges payable in respect of the weighing of cattle, sheep or
swine shall be paid in advance to an authorised market officer by the
person bringing the animals to be weighed.'

6. In section 56(1) (prohibited sales in market hours), for the word 'district'
there shall be substituted the word 'area'.

7. In section 57 (weighing machines and scales), subsection (1) shall cease
to have effect.

8. After that section there shall be inserted the following section—
'57A. Provision of cold stores.
(1) A market authority may provide a cold air store or refrigerator for
the storage and preservation of meat and other articles of food.

(2) Any proposal by a market authority to provide under this section
a cold air store or refrigerator within the area of another local authority
requires the consent of that other authority, which shall not be unreasonably withheld.

(3) Any question whether or not such a consent is unreasonably
withheld shall be referred to and determined by the Ministers.

(4) Subsections (1) to (5) of section 250 of the Local Government Act
1972 (which relate to local inquiries) shall apply for the purposes of this
section as if any reference in those subsections to that Act included a
reference to this section.'

9. Section 58 (weighing of articles) shall cease to have effect.

10. In section 60 (market byelaws), after paragraph (c) there shall be
inserted the following paragraph—

'(d) after consulting the fire authority for the area in which the market
is situated, for preventing the spread of fires in the market.'

11. In section 61 (interpretation of Part III), the words from 'and this Part'
to the end shall cease to have effect and for the definition of 'market authority'
there shall be substituted the following definitions—

'"fire authority" means an authority exercising the functions of a fire
authority under the Fire Services Act 1947;

"food" has the same meaning as in the Food Safety Act 1990;

"local authority" means a district council, a London borough council or
a parish or community council;

"market authority" means a local authority who maintain a market which
has been established or acquired under section 50(1) or under the
corresponding provisions of any earlier enactment.'

Amendments of Part V

12.   Part V of the 1984 Act (sugar beet and cold storage) shall be amended in accordance with paragraphs 13 to 16 below.

13.—(1)   In subsections (1) and (2) of section 68 (research and education), for the word 'Company', wherever it occurs, there shall be substituted the words 'processors of home-grown beet'.

(2)   After subsection (5) of that section there shall be inserted the following subsection—

'(5A)   An order under this section shall be made by statutory instrument which shall be subject to annulment in pursuance of a resolution of either House of Parliament.'.

(3)   In subsection (6) of that section, for the definition of 'the Company' and subsequent definitions there shall be substituted—

'"year" means a period of 12 months beginning with 1st April;
and in this section and section 69 and 69A "home-grown beet" means sugar beet grown in Great Britain'.

14.   In subsection (3) of section 69 (crop price), for the words '"home-grown beet" means sugar beet grown in Great Britain; and' there shall be substituted the words 'and section 69A'.

15.   After that section there shall be inserted the following section—
'69A. Information.

(1)   For the purpose of facilitating—

(a)   the making of a determination under section 69(1); or

(b)   the preparation or conduct of discussions concerning Community arrangements for or relating to the regulation of the market for sugar,

the appropriate Minister may serve on any processor of home-grown beet a notice requiring him to furnish in writing, within such period as is specified in the notice, such information as is so specified.

(2)   Subject to subsection (3), information obtained under subsection (1) shall not be disclosed without the previous consent in writing of the person by whom the information was furnished; and a person who discloses any information so obtained in contravention of this subsection shall be liable—

(a)   on conviction on indictment, to a fine or to imprisonment for a term not exceeding two years or to both;

(b)   on summary conviction, to a fine not exceeding the statutory maximum or to imprisonment for a term not exceeding three months or to both.

(3)   Nothing in subsection (2) shall restrict the disclosure of information to any of the Ministers or the disclosure—

(a)   of information obtained under subsection (1)(a)—

(i)   to a person designated to make a determination under section 69(1); or

(ii)   to a body which substantially represents the growers of home-grown beet; or

(b) of information obtained under subsection (1)(b), to the Community institution concerned.

(4) In this section 'the appropriate Minister' means—

(a) in relation to England, the Minister of Agriculture, Fisheries and Food; and

(b) in relation to Scotland or Wales, the Secretary of State.'

16. Section 70 (provision of cold storage) shall cease to have effect.

Section 59(1).   SCHEDULE 3

MINOR AND CONSEQUENTIAL AMENDMENTS

The Public Health Act 1936 (c. 49)

1. An order made by the Secretary of State under section 6 of the Public Health Act 1936 may constitute a united district for the purposes of any functions under this Act which are functions of a food authority in England and Wales.

The London Government Act 1963 (c. 33)

2. Section 54(1) of the London Government Act 1963 (food, drugs, markets and animals) shall cease to have effect.

The Agriculture Act 1967 (c. 22)

3. In section 7(3) of the Agriculture Act 1967 (labelling of meat in relation to systems of classifying meat), the words from 'and, without prejudice' to the end shall cease to have effect.

4.—(1) In subsection (2) of section 25 of that Act (interpretation of Part I), for the definition of 'slaughterhouse' there shall be substituted the following definition—

'"slaughterhouse" has, in England and Wales, the meaning given by section 34 of the Slaughterhouses Act 1974 and, in Scotland, the meaning given by section 22 of the Slaughter of Animals (Scotland) Act 1980;'.

(2) In subsection (3) of that section, for the words from 'Part II' to '1955' there shall be substituted the words 'section 15 of the Slaughterhouses Act 1974 or section 1 of the Slaughter of Animals (Scotland) Act 1980'.

The Farm and Garden Chemicals Act 1967 (c. 50)

5. In section 4 of the Farm and Garden Chemicals Act 1967 (evidence of analysis of products)—

(a) in subsection (3), for the words 'section 76 of the Food Act 1984' there shall be substituted the words 'section 27 of the Food Safety Act 1990'; and

(b) in subsection (7)(c), the words from 'for the reference' to '1956' shall cease to have effect.

The Trade Descriptions Act 1968 (c. 29)

6.   In section 2(5)(a) of the Trade Descriptions Act 1968 (certain descriptions to be deemed not to be trade descriptions), for the words 'the Food Act 1984, the Food and Drugs (Scotland) Act 1956' there shall be substituted the words 'the Food Safety Act 1990'.

7.   In section 22 of that Act (admissibility of evidence in proceedings for offences under Act), in subsection (2), the paragraph beginning with the words 'In this subsection' shall cease to have effect, and after that subsection there shall be inserted the following subsection—

'(2A)   In subsection (2) of this section—
"the food and drugs laws" means the Food Safety Act 1990, the Medicines Act 1968 and the Food (Northern Ireland) Order 1989 and any instrument made thererunder;
"the relevant provisions" means—
(i)   in relation to the said Act of 1990, section 31 and regulations made thereunder;
(ii)   in relation to the said Act of 1968, so much of Schedule 3 to that Act as is applicable to the circumstances in which the sample was procured; and
(iii)   in relation to the said Order, Articles 40 and 44,
or any provisions replacing any of those provisions by virtue of section 17 of the said Act of 1990, paragraph 27 of Schedule 3 to the said Act of 1968 or Article 72 or 73 of the said Order.'

The Medicines Act 1968 (c. 67)

8.   In section 108 of the Medicines Act 1968 (enforcement in England and Wales)—
(a)   for the words 'food and drugs authority', in each place where they occur, there shall be substituted the words 'drugs authority'; and
(b)   after subsection (11) there shall be inserted the following subsection—

'(12)   In this section "drugs authority" means—
(a)   as respects each London borough, metropolitan district or non-metropolitan county, the council of that borough, district or county; and
(b)   as respects the City of London (including the Temples), the Common Council of that City.'

9.   In section 109 of that Act (enforcement in Scotland)—
(a)   paragraph (c) of subsection (2) shall cease to have effect; and
(b)   after that subsection there shall be inserted the following subsection—

'(2A)   Subsection (12) of section 108 of this Act shall have effect in relation to Scotland as if for paragraphs (a) and (b) there were substituted the words "an islands or district council"'.

10.   After section 115 of that Act there shall be inserted the following section—

'115A.   Facilities for microbiological examinations.

A drugs authority or the council of a non-metropolican district may provide facilities for microbiological examinations of drugs.'

11.   In section 132(1) of that Act (interpretation), the definition of 'food and drugs authority' shall cease to have effect and after the definition of 'doctor' there shall be inserted the following definition—

'"drugs authority" has the meaning assigned to it by section 108(12) of this Act;'.

12.   In paragraph 1(2) of Schedule 3 to that Act (sampling) for the words from 'in relation to England and Wales' to 'Food and Drugs (Scotland) Act 1956' there shall be substituted the words 'except in relation to Northern Ireland, has the meaning assigned to it by section 27 of the Food Safety Act 1990'.

The Transport Act 1968 (c. 73)

13.   In Schedule 16 to the Transport Act 1968 (supplementary and consequential provisions), in paragraph 7(2), paragraphs (d) and (e) shall cease to have effect.

The Tribunals and Inquiries Act 1971 (c. 62)

14.—(1)   In Schedule 1 to the Tribunals and Inquiries Act 1971 (tribunals under supervision of Council on Tribunals), paragraph 15 shall cease to have effect and after paragraph 6B there shall be inserted the following paragraph—

'Food	6C. Tribunals constituted in accordance with regulations under Part II of the Food Safety Act 1990.'

(2)   In that Schedule, paragraph 40 shall cease to have effect and after paragraph 36 there shall be inserted the following paragraph—

'Food	36A. Tribunals constituted in accordance with regulations under Part II of the Food Safety Act 1990 being tribunals appointed for Scotland.'

The Agriculture (Miscellaneous Provisions) Act 1972 (c. 62)

15.—(1)   In subsection (1) of section 4 of the Agriculture (Miscellaneous Provisions) Act 1972 (furnishing by milk marketing boards of information derived from tests of milk)—

(a)   for the words 'appropriate authority' there shall be substituted the words 'enforcement authority'; and

(b)   for the words from 'Milk and Dairies Regulations' to '1956' there shall be substituted the words 'regulations relating to milk, dairies or dairy farms which were made under, or have effect as if made under, section 16 of the Food Safety Act 1990.'

(2)   In subsection (2) of that section, for the definition of 'appropriate authority' there shall be substituted the following definition—

'"enforcement authority" has the same meaning as in the Food Safety Act 1990;'.

(3)   Subsection (3) of that section shall cease to have effect.

The Poisons Act 1972 (c. 66)

16.   In section 8(4)(a) of the Poisons Act 1972 (evidence of analysis in proceedings under Act) for the words 'section 76 of the Food Act 1984, or section 27 of the Food and Drugs (Scotland) Act 1956' there shall be substituted the words 'section 27 of the Food Safety Act 1990'.

The Local Government Act 1972 (c. 70)

17.   In section 259(3) of the Local Government Act 1972 (compensation for loss of office)—

(a)   in paragraph (b), for the words 'food and drugs authority, within the meaning of the Food Act 1984' there shall be substituted the words 'food authority within the meaning of the Food Safety Act 1990';

(b)   in paragraph (c), for sub-paragraphs (i) and (ii) there shall be substituted the words 'which are incorporated or reproduced in the Slaughterhouses Act 1974 or the Food Safety Act 1990'; and

(c)   the words 'section 129(1) of the Food and Drugs Act 1955' shall cease to have effect.

The Slaughterhouses Act 1974 (c. 3)

18.   In the following provisions of the Slaughterhouses Act 1974, namely—

(a)   section 2(2)(a) (requirements to be complied with in relation to slaughterhouse licences);

(b)   section 4(2)(a) (requirements to be complied with in relation to knacker's yard licences);

(c)   section 12(2) (regulations with respect to slaughterhouses and knackers' yards to prevail over byelaws); and

(d)   section 16(3) (regulations with respect to public slaughterhouses to prevail over byelaws),

for the words 'section 13 of the Food Act 1984' there shall be substituted the words 'section 16 of the Food Safety Act 1990'.

The Licensing (Scotland) Act 1976 (c. 66)

19.   In section 23(4) of the Licensing (Scotland) Act 1976 (application for new licence), for the words 'section 13 of the Food and Drugs (Scotland) Act 1956' there shall be substituted 'section 16 of the Food Safety Act 1990'.

The Weights and Measures &c. Act 1976 (c. 77)

20.—(1)   In subsection (1) of section 12 of the Weights and Measures &c. Act 1976 (shortages of food and other goods), for paragraphs (a) and (b) there shall be substituted the following paragraph—

'(a)   section 16 of the Food Safety Act 1990 ("the 1990 Act");'.

(2)   In subsection (9) of that section—

(a) for paragraph (a) there shall be substituted the following paragraph—
    '(a) where it was imposed under the 1990 Act—
        (i) the Minister of Agriculture, Fisheries and Food and the Secre-
tary of State acting jointly in so far as it was imposed in relation to
England and Wales; and
        (ii) the Secretary of State in so far as it was imposed in relation to
Scotland;'; and
    (b) in paragraph (c), the words 'the 1956 Act or' shall cease to have
effect.

21. In Schedule 6 to that Act (temporary requirements imposed by
emergency orders), for paragraphs 2 and 3 there shall be substituted the
following paragraph—

'Food Safety Act 1990 (c. 16)

2.—(1) This paragraph applies where the relevant requirement took
effect under or by virtue of the Food Safety Act 1990.
    (2) The following provisions of that Act—
        (a) Part I (preliminary);
        (b) Part III (administration and enforcement); and
        (c) sections 40 to 50 (default powers and other supplemental provi-
sions),
shall apply as if the substituted requirement were imposed by regulations
under section 16 of that Act.'

The Hydrocarbon Oil Duties Act 1979 (c. 5)

22. In Schedule 5 to the Hydrocarbon Oil Duties Act 1979 (sampling) in
paragraph 5(d) for the words 'section 76 of the Food Act 1984, section 27 of
the Food and Drugs (Scotland) Act 1956' there shall be substituted the words
'section 27 of the Food Safety Act 1990'.

The Slaughter of Animals (Scotland) Act 1980 (c. 13)

23. In section 19(2) of the Slaughter of Animals (Scotland) Act 1980
(enforcement) for the words 'section 13 of the Food and Drugs (Scotland) Act
1956' there shall be substituted the words 'section 16 of the Food Safety Act
1990' and for the words 'section 36 of the said Act of 1956' there shall be
substituted the words 'section 32 of the said Act of 1990'.

24. In section 22 of that Act (interpretation)—
    (a) for the definition of 'knacker's yard' there shall be substituted the
following definition—
        '"knacker's yard" means any premises used in connection with the
        business of slaughtering, flaying or cutting up animals the flesh of which
        is not intended for human consumption; and "knacker" means a person
        whose business it is to carry out such slaughtering, flaying or cutting up';
and
    (b) for the definition of 'slaughterhouse' there shall be substituted the
following definition—

'"slaughterhouse" means a place for slaughtering animals, the flesh of which is intended for human consumption, and includes any place available in connection with such a place for the confinement of animals while awaiting slaughter there or keeping, or subjecting to any treatment or process, products of the slaughtering of animals there; and "slaughterman" means a person whose business it is to carry out such slaughtering'.

The Civic Government (Scotland) Act 1982 (c. 45)

25. In section 39 of the Civic Government (Scotland) Act 1982 (street traders' licences)—

(a) in subsection (3)(b), for the words 'section 7 of the Milk and Dairies (Scotland) Act 1914' there shall be substituted the words 'regulations made under section 19 of the Food Safety Act 1990'; and

(b) in subsection (4)—

(i) for the words 'regulations made under sections 13 and 56 of the Food and Drugs (Scotland) Act 1956', there shall be substituted the words 'section 1(3) of the Food Safety Act 1990';

(ii) for the words 'islands or district council' there shall be substituted the words 'food authority (for the purposes of section 5 of the Food Safety Act 1990)'; and

(iii) for the words 'sections 13 and 56 of the Food and Drugs (Scotland) Act 1956', there shall be substituted the words 'section 16 of the Food Safety Act 1990'.

The Public Health (Control of Disease) Act 1984 (c. 22)

26. In section 3(2) of the Public Health (Control of Disease) Act 1984 (jurisdiction and powers of port health authority), for paragraph (a) there shall be substituted the following paragraph—

'(a) of a food authority under the Food Safety Act 1990;'.

27. In section 7(3) of that Act (London port health authority), for paragraph (d) there shall be substituted the following paragraph—

'(d) of a food authority under any provision of the Food Safety Act 1990.'

28.—(1) In subsection (1) of section 20 of that Act (stopping of work to prevent spread of disease), in paragraph (b) for the words 'subsection (1) of section 28 of the Food Act 1984' there shall be substituted 'subsection (1A) below'.

(2) After that subsection there shall be inserted the following subsection—

'(1A) The diseases to which this subsection applies are—

(a) enteric fever (including typhoid and paratyphoid fevers);

(b) dysentery;

(c) diphtheria;

(d) scarlet fever;

(e) acute inflammation of the throat;

(f) gastro-enteritis; and

(g) undulant fever.'

The Food and Environment Protection Act 1985 (c. 48)

29. In section 24(1) of the Food and Environment Protection Act 1985 (interpretation)—
    (a) in the definition of 'designated incident', for the words 'designated incident' there shall be substituted the words 'designated circumstances';
    (b) the definition of 'escape' shall cease to have effect; and
    (c) for the definition of 'food' there shall be substituted—
    '"food" has the same meaning as in the Food Safety Act 1990'.

30. In section 25 of that Act (Northern Ireland) after subsection (4) there shall be inserted the following subsection—
    '(4A) Section 24(1) above shall have effect in relation to Northern Ireland as if for the definition of "food" there were substituted the following definition—
    '"food' has the meaning assigned to it by Article 2(2) of the Food (Northern Ireland) Order 1989, except that it includes water which is bottled or is an ingredient of food;".'

The Local Government Act 1985 (c. 51)

31. In paragraph 15 of Schedule 8 to the Local Government Act 1985 (trading standards and related functions)—
    (a) sub-paragraph (2) shall cease to have effect; and
    (b) at the end of sub-paragraph (6) there shall be added the words 'or section 5(1) of the Food Safety Act 1990'.

The Weights and Measures Act 1985 (c. 72)

32. In section 38 of the Weights and Measures Act 1985 (special powers of inspectors), subsection (4) (exclusion for milk) shall cease to have effect.

33. In section 93 of that Act (powers under other Acts with respect to marking of food) for the words 'Food Act 1984' there shall be substituted the words 'Food Safety Act 1990'.

34. In section 94(1) of that Act (interpretation), in the definition of 'drugs' and 'food' for the words 'Food Act 1984, or, in Scotland, the Food and Drugs (Scotland) Act 1956' there shall be substituted the words 'Food Safety Act 1990'.

The Agriculture Act 1986 (c. 49)

35. In section 1(6) of the Agriculture Act 1986 (provision of agricultural goods and services), in the definition of 'food', for the words 'Food Act 1984' there shall be substituted 'Food Safety Act 1990'.

The National Health Service (Amendment) Act 1986 (c. 66)

36.—(1) In subsection (2) of section 1 of the National Health Service (Amendment) Act 1986 (application of food legislation to health authorities and health service premises)—

(a)   for the words 'appropriate authority' there shall be substituted the word 'Ministers'; and

(b)   for the word 'authority' there shall be substituted the word 'Ministers'.

(2)   For subsection (7) of that section there shall be substituted—

'(7)   In this section—

"the Ministers" has the same meanining as in the Food Safety Act 1990;

"the food legislation" means the Food Safety Act 1990 and any regulations or orders made (or having effect as if made) under it;

"health authority"—

(a)   as respects England and Wales, has the meaning assigned to it by section 128 of the 1977 Act; and

(b)   as respects Scotland, means a Health Board constituted under section 2 of the 1978 Act, the Common Services Agency constituted under section 10 of that Act or a State Hospital Management Committee constituted under section 91 of the Mental Health (Scotland) Act 1984.'

The Consumer Protection Act 1987 (c. 43)

37.   In section 19(1) of the Consumer Protection Act 1987 (interpretation of Part II), in the definition of 'food' for the words 'Food Act 1984' there shall be substituted 'Food Safety Act 1990'.

The Road Traffic Offenders Act 1988 (c. 53)

38.   In section 16(7) of the Road Traffic Offenders Act 1988 (meaning of 'authorised analyst' in relation to proceedings under Act), for the words 'section 76 of the Food Act 1984, or section 27 of the Food and Drugs (Scotland) Act 1956' there shall be substituted the words 'section 27 of the Food Safety Act 1990'.

SCHEDULE 4

TRANSITIONAL PROVISIONS AND SAVINGS

Ships and aircraft

1.   In relation to any time before the commencement of the first order under section 1(3) of this Act—

(a)   any ship which is a home-going ship within the meanining of section 132 of the 1984 Act or section 58 of the 1956 Act (interpretation) shall be regarded as premises for the purposes of this Act; and

(b)   the powers of entry conferred by section 32 of this Act shall include the right to enter any ship or aircraft for the purpose of ascertaining whether there is in the ship or aircraft any food imported as part of the cargo in contravention of the provisions of regulations made under Part II of this Act; and in this Act as it applies by virtue of this paragraph 'occupier', in relation to any ship or aircraft, means the master, commander or other person in charge of the ship or aircraft.

Regulations under the 1984 Act

2.—(1) In so far as any existing regulations made, or having effect as if made, under any provision of the 1984 Act specified in the first column of Table A below have effect in relation to England and Wales, they shall have effect, after the commencement of the relevant repeal, as if made under the provisions of this Act specified in relation to that provision in the second column of that Table, or such of those provisions as are applicable.

(2) In this paragraph and paragraph 3 and 4 below 'existing regulations' means—

(a) any regulations made, or having effect as if made, under a provision repealed by this Act; and

(b) any orders having effect as if made under such regulations, which are in force immediately before the coming into force of that repeal; and references to the commencement of the relevant repeal shall be construed accordingly.

TABLE A

Provision of the 1984 Act	Provision of this Act
section 4 (composition etc. of food)	sections 16(1)(a), (c) and (f) and (3) and 17(1)
section 7 (describing food)	section 16(1)(e)
section 13 (food hygiene)	section 16(1)(b), (c), (d) and (f), (2) and (3)
section 33 (milk and dairies)	section 16(1)(b), (c), (d) and (f), (2) and (3)
section 34 (registration), so far as relating to dairies or dairy farms	section 19
section 38 (milk: special designations)	section 18(2)
section 73(2) (qualification of officers)	section 5(6)
section 76(2) (public analysts)	section 27(2)
section 79(5) (form of certificate)	section 49(2)
section 119 (Community provisions)	section 17(2)

Regulations under the 1956 Act

3. Any existing regulations made, or having effect as if made, under any provision of the 1956 Act specified in the first column of Table B below shall have effect, after the commencement of the relevant repeal, as if made under the provisions of this Act specified in relation to that provision in the second column of that Table, or such of those provisions as are applicable.

TABLE B

Provision of the 1956 Act	Provision of this Act
section 4 (composition etc. of food)	sections 16(1)(a), (c) and (f) and (3) and 17(1)
section 7 (describing food)	section 16(1)(e)
section 13 (food hygiene)	sections 5(6) and 16(1)(b), (c), (d) and (f), (2) and (3)
section 16(2) (regulations as to milk)	section 18(2)
section 27(2) (public analysts)	section 27(2)
section 29(3) (form of certificate)	section 49(2)
section 56A (Community provisions)	section 17(2)

Other regulations

4. In so far as any existing regulations made under section 1 of the Importation of Milk Act 1983 have effect in relation to Great Britain, they shall have effect, after the commencement of the relevant repeal, as if made under section 18(1)(b) of this Act.

Orders with respect to milk in Scotland

5.—(1) Any existing order made under section 12(2) of the Milk and Dairies (Scotland) Act 1914 (orders with respect to milk) shall have effect, after the commencement of the relevant repeal, as if it were regulations made under section 16(1)(b), (d) and (f) and (2) of this Act.

(2) Any existing order made under section 3 of the Milk and Dairies (Amendment) Act 1922 (sale of milk under special designations) shall have effect, after the commencement of the relevant repeal, as if it were regulations made under section 18(2) of this Act.

(3) In this paragraph 'existing order' means any order made under a provision repealed by this Act which is in force immediately before the coming into force of that repeal; and references to the commencement of the relevant repeal shall be construed accordingly.

Disqualification orders

6. The repeal by this Act of section 14 of the 1984 Act (court's power to disqualify caterers) shall not have effect as respects any order made, or having effect as if made, under that section which is in force immediately before the commencement of that repeal.

Food hygiene byelaws

7.—(1) The repeal by this Act of section 15 of the 1984 Act (byelaws as to food) shall not have effect as respects any byelaws made, or having effect as if made, under that section which are in force immediately before the commencement of that repeal.

(2) In so far as any such byelaws conflict with any regulations made, or having effect as if made, under Part II of this Act, the regulations shall prevail.

Closure orders

8.   The repeal by this Act of section 21 of the 1984 Act or section 1 of the Control of Food Premises (Scotland) Act 1977 (closure orders) shall not have effect as respects any order made, or having effect as if made, under that section which is in force immediately before the commencement of that repeal.

Section 59(4).   **SCHEDULE 5**

REPEALS

Chapter	Short title	Extent of repeal
1914 c. 46.	The Milk and Dairies (Scotland) Act 1914.	The whole Act.
1922 c. 54.	The Milk and Dairies (Amendment) Act 1922.	The whole Act.
1934 c. 51.	The Milk Act 1934.	The whole Act.
1949 c. 34.	The Milk (Special Designations) Act 1949.	The whole Act.
1956 c. 30.	The Food and Drugs (Scotland) Act 1956.	The whole Act.
1963 c. 33.	The London Government Act 1963.	Section 54(1).
1967 c. 22.	The Agriculture Act 1967.	In section 7(3), the words from 'and, without prejudice' to the end.
1967 c. 50.	The Farm and Garden Chemicals Act 1967.	In section 4(7)(c), the words from 'for the reference' to '1956'.
1968 c. 29.	The Trade Descriptions Act 1968.	In section 22(2), the paragraph beginning with the words 'In this subsection'.
1968 c. 67.	The Medicines Act 1968.	In section 132(1), the definition of 'food and drugs authority'. In Schedule 5, paragraph 17.
1968 c. 73.	The Transport Act 1968.	In Schedule 16, in paragraph 7(2), paragraphs (d) and (e).
1971 c. 62.	The Tribunals and Inquiries Act 1971.	In Schedule 1, paragraphs 15 and 40.
1972 c. 66.	The Agriculture (Miscellaneous Provisions) Act 1972.	Section 4(3).

Chapter	Short title	Extent of repeal
1972 c. 68.	The European Communities Act 1972.	In Schedule 4, paragraph 3(2)(c).
1976 c. 77.	The Weights and Measures &c. Act 1976.	In section 12(9)(c), the words 'the 1956 Act or'.
1977 c. 28.	The Control of Food Premises (Scotland) Act 1977.	The whole Act.
1983 c. 37.	The Importation of Milk Act 1983.	The whole Act.
1984 c. 30.	The Food Act 1984.	Parts I and II. In section 51(2), the word 'market'. In section 53, in subsection (1) the words 'and in respect of the weighing and measuring of articles and vehicles', and in subsection (3)(b) the words 'in respect of the weighing of vehicles, or as the case may be,' Section 57(1). Section 58. In section 61, the words from 'and this Part' to the end. Part IV. Sections 70 to 92. In section 93, in subsection (2), paragraphs (b) to (d) and, in subsection (3), paragraphs (a) to (e) and (h) to (l). In section 94, subsection (1) except as regards offences under Part III of the Act, and subsection (2). In section 95, subsections (2) to (8). Sections 96 to 109. Sections 111 to 120. In section 121, subsections (2) and (3). Sections 122 to 131.

Chapter	Short title	Extent of repeal
		In section 132, subsection (1) except the words 'In this Act, unless the context otherwise requires' and the definitions of 'animal' and 'the Minister'. Sections 133 and 134. In section 136, in subsection (2), paragraphs (b) and (c). Schedules 1 to 11.
1985 c. 48.	The Food and Environment Protection Act 1985.	In section 1(2), the definition of 'escape'. In section 24(1), the definition of 'escape'.
1985 c. 51.	The Local Government Act 1985.	In Schedule 8, paragraph 15(2).
1985 c. 72.	The Weights and Measures Act 1985.	Section 38(4).

Index